JB
A5491B78

D0896973

THE LIFE OF
MARIAN
ANDERSON

Diva and
Humanitarian

Series Consultant:
Dr. Russell L. Adams, Chairman
Department of Afro-American Studies, Howard University

Andrea Broadwater

Enslow Publishers, Inc.
40 Industrial Road
Box 398
Berkeley Heights, NJ 07922
USA

http://www.enslow.com

DETROIT PUBLIC LIBRARY
5201 WOODWARD AVE.
DETROIT, MI 48202
CL

This book is dedicated to my nieces and nephews.

ACKNOWLEDGMENTS

I would like to thank the following for their invaluable assistance: Walter Dean Myers; The Harlem Writers Guild; The Van Pelt-Dietrich Library at the University of Pennsylvania

Copyright © 2015 by Andrea Broadwater

All rights reserved.

Originally published as *Marian Anderson: Singer and Humanitarian* in 2000.

No part of this book may be reproduced by any means without the written permission of the publisher.

Library of Congress Cataloging-in-Publication Data

Broadwater, Andrea.
    The life of Marian Anderson : diva and humanitarian / Andrea Broadwater.
       pages cm. — (Legendary African Americans)
    Includes bibliographical references and index.
    ISBN 978-0-7660-6285-6
    1. Anderson, Marian, 1897–1993—Juvenile literature. 2. Contraltos—United States—Biography—Juvenile literature. 3. African American singers—Biography—Juvenile literature.
    I. Title.
    ML3930.A5B76 2015
    782.1092—dc23
    [B]
                         2014027444

Future editions:
Paperback ISBN: 978-0-7660-6286-3   EPUB ISBN: 978-0-7660-6287-0
Single-User PDF ISBN: 978-0-7660-6288-7   Multi-User PDF ISBN: 978-0-7660-6289-4

Printed in the United States of America
102014 Bang Printing, Brainerd, Minn.
10 9 8 7 6 5 4 3 2 1

To Our Readers:
We have done our best to make sure all Internet addresses in this book were active and appropriate when we went to press. However, the author and the publisher have no control over and assume no liability for the material available on those Internet sites or on other Web sites they may link to. Any comments or suggestions can be sent by e-mail to comments@enslow.com or to the address on the back cover.

♻ Enslow Publishers, Inc., is committed to printing our books on recycled paper. The paper in every book contains 10% to 30% post-consumer waste (PCW). The cover board on the outside of each book contains 100% PCW. Our goal is to do our part to help young people and the environment too!

Illustration Credits: Library of Congress, page 4

Cover Illustration: Library of Congress

CONTENTS

Marian Anderson sings "The Star-Spangled Banner" at the dedication of a mural commemorating her free public concert on the steps of the Lincoln Memorial on Easter Sunday, 1939. The dedication took place on January 6, 1943.

Chapter 1

TOWN HALL— A LEAP FORWARD

O n the night of December 30, 1935, the curtains opened on the stage of Town Hall in downtown New York City. The audience was startled by what it saw.[1] The young singer was already standing onstage, posed behind the concert piano. This was surprising because singers usually walked onto the stage after the curtains opened. In her black-and-gold brocade gown, Marian Anderson leaned against the piano for support. She knew that her unexpected appearance onstage may have seemed dramatic to the audience, and she was fearful of what they were thinking of her.[2] But Anderson also knew that underneath the long beautiful dress, a plaster cast covered her left leg from her foot to her knee. Unknown to the audience, just weeks before her recital she had fallen and had broken her ankle. In one of the most important performances of her life, Anderson would have to sing with her painful leg in a cast.

For many reasons, this concert had to succeed. Eleven years earlier Anderson had performed at Town Hall with devastating results. Until then, Anderson had sung mostly for African-American audiences. In 1924, as her audiences began to widen, she decided to take a risk and stage a recital in New York City's Town Hall. That recital pulled her career a step back instead of pushing it ahead.

▲ ▲ ▲

From the beginning, Anderson had sensed trouble when the concert manager held up the 1924 performance for an hour. When she stepped out on the stage at Town Hall, she saw why. Only a small number of people had shown up to hear her sing. For the program, Anderson had selected four German art songs—called *lieder*—to sing. She had chosen those songs because a famous classical singer, Roland Hayes, included *lieder* in his programs. Anderson admired Hayes, and she wanted to sing *lieder* too. But there was one problem: Anderson could not speak German. She sang the German songs phonetically—by the sounds of the words. As Anderson struggled with the German language, the audience noticed it.

Feeling lost and defeated, Anderson returned to her home in Philadelphia. For months after the concert, she moped around the house. She even considered abandoning her singing career. Eventually, she recovered from the blow with the help of her mother's advice. Anderson's mother said, "Whatever you do in this world, no matter how good it is, you will never be able to please everybody. All you can strive for is to do the best it is humanly possible for you to do."[3]

Anderson came to realize that more than anything else, she wanted to be a classical singer. She loved to sing the spirituals she had sung in church as a child. She also loved to sing the classical French, Italian, and German songs. Yet, to sing them properly she had to master these foreign languages. And the only place to do that was Europe. Despite having little money, Anderson resolved to sail for Europe. She resolved that there would be no more embarrassing moments for her.

Anderson traveled to Europe several times. Her first trip ended abruptly when her famous vocal teacher, Raimund von Zur Mühlen, suddenly fell ill. On her second trip, she met a Finnish pianist, Kosti Vehanen. Vehanen became a longtime friend and the accompanist for her concerts. He spoke German and tutored her in the language.

On her third trip to Europe, Anderson met Sol Hurok, a well-known impresario, or manager. He managed the careers of many famous people. When Hurok heard Anderson sing at a Paris concert, he offered to represent her in the United States.

During this time in the United States, there were laws, known as Jim Crow laws, designed to keep black and white people in "separate but equal" facilities. Places such as movie theaters, trains, bathrooms, and even drinking fountains were supposed to be "separate but equal." Although the places were separate, they were not at all equal. The places for African Americans were usually in an inferior condition. Those segregation laws ruled the South, and racism ruled the land. For this reason, despite her singing talent, many doors were closed to Marian Anderson just because she was African American. Anderson hoped that Hurok, known for his bold management, could advance her career.

As her new manager, Sol Hurok scheduled the 1935 Town Hall concert. The concert, her first after a successful tour in Europe, would be a major turning point in her career if she gave a winning performance. Hurok stated, "I knew I would have no difficulty filling her schedule after she had sung in Town Hall."[4]

Anderson and her accompanist, Vehanen, carefully selected the songs for the program. On the ship back to the United States, they rehearsed each song for hours. Everything seemed to be smooth sailing—that is, until Anderson tumbled down the stairs and broke her ankle.

The accident alarmed everyone. Anderson, however, was determined to sing, so she and Vehanen devised a plan.[5] A registered nurse accompanied her to New York to tend to her ankle. Anderson stayed at the YWCA uptown in Harlem. Although a hotel closer to Town Hall would have been more convenient, no hotel would rent her a room because of her race. Fortunately, on the day of the concert, a white admirer offered her the use of a suite in a downtown hotel. Although the hotel manager gave her a cool reception, Anderson was able to stay there for two nights.

With that problem solved, Anderson faced the next one. How could she get on and off the stage without the audience seeing the cast? Anderson flatly refused to inform the press or the audience about her injury. She did not want sympathy from the audience. She wanted their thoughts to be on her art alone.[6]

As planned, stagehands lowered the curtains before the concert and brought Anderson to the stage in a wheelchair. Vehanen and the nurse helped her to the side of the piano, where she was standing when the curtains opened. Fearful but hopeful, Anderson faced the large audience with the long evening gown hiding her leg cast.

Now just one more hurdle remained. The first song, George Handel's "Begrüssung," began with a long, difficult note. Anderson knew that the first note of the first song made a decisive impression on the audience. So much depended on this one note. She ignored the pain in her ankle. As friends and family in the audience watched,

Anderson thought of the hours she had spent singing this note. She closed her eyes and took a deep breath. Recalling her mother's advice, she opened her mouth and sang the best she could. The loud applause after the song dispelled all her fears. Midway through the performance, she explained the injury and cast to the audience, and they only applauded more.

Although some critics were reserved with their praise, one reviewer for *The New York Times* wrote, "Let it be said at the outset: Marian Anderson has returned to her native land one of the great singers of our time."[7]

Unlike her first performance at Town Hall, this performance was no step backward. Anderson stated, "If there has been one appearance that seemed like a leap forward, this Town Hall event was it."[8]

In the years to come, despite the heavy cast of racism, there would be many leaps forward for this talented and determined young woman who came from humble beginnings in South Philadelphia, Pennsylvania.

Chapter 2

BABY CONTRALTO

W e were poor folk. But there was a wealth in our poverty, a wealth of music and love and faith," said Marian Anderson of her childhood.[1] On February 27, 1897, Marian was born to Anna and John Anderson in South Philadelphia, Pennsylvania.[2] They lived in a rented room on Webster Street for two years until Marian's sister Alyce was born. The family then moved in with Marian's paternal grandparents on Fitzwater Street. With the birth of her youngest sister, Ethel, the family moved into a house on Colorado Street, not far from Marian's grandparents.

The rented house lacked a real bathroom, so Anna Anderson scrubbed her daughters in a large wooden tub placed in the center of the kitchen. Marian loved to spend time in the kitchen with her mother. Sometimes she sat at the table and tapped out a beat. She liked to sing made-up melodies.

Anna Delilah Anderson, a short, quiet woman, was a former schoolteacher from Lynchburg, Virginia. John Berkeley Anderson, a tall and proud man, worked at various jobs to support his family. He worked in the refrigerator room at the Reading Terminal Market in downtown Philadelphia, and he also had a small business selling ice and coal.

John Anderson loved to plan and prepare picnics for his three daughters.[3] The girls enjoyed going on family outings, which sometimes included hayrides. Anderson and her sisters played with the other neighborhood children in games such as hopscotch, jacks, and follow-the-leader. On Sundays, the Anderson sisters also liked to go to church with their father. John Anderson often took his daughters to Union Baptist Church, where he was in charge of the ushers. The girls also visited the Methodist church that their mother attended.

The pastor of Union Baptist Church, the Reverend Wesley G. Parks, had a deep appreciation for music and often presented concerts with well-known singers and musicians. And what a perfect place for Marian Anderson to be! At a very young age, she showed a fascination for music. In school, she would listen to the music class next door to her classroom and learn the songs through the wall.[4]

One day John Anderson brought home a used piano for the family. Excitement and joy filled the Anderson home. Her parents could not afford piano lessons, so Marian obtained a sheet with the musical notes of the keyboard. She placed the sheet behind the keys and taught herself to play a few melodies. The Andersons often had family sings, and they would harmonize together. Mostly they sang spirituals because, as Marian Anderson later explained, "they were the easiest and everybody seemed to know the tunes and words."[5] While walking down the street one day, young Marian heard beautiful music from a nearby house. She peeped through the window and saw an African-American woman playing the piano. When Marian saw the woman with dark skin like hers, she believed that she too could learn to play as well.[6]

Then another musical instrument caught her attention. At a concert, Marian heard a violinist play a solo. She became inspired to play the violin too. She knew, though, that a violin cost a lot of money. One way to earn money in her neighborhood was to scrub the doorsteps for five or ten cents. Marian scrubbed her neighbors' steps until she had saved enough money to purchase a used violin, which she had seen in a neighborhood pawnshop. Although the shopkeeper assured her that it was a good one, the strings broke and the bridge collapsed when she played it. Marian never really learned to play the violin. Other interests also held her attention, like the ballet. Holding the back of a chair for balance, she tried to stand on her toes in a pair of used ballet slippers without falling on her face. The high point of her dance experience was dancing in a chorus line with a group of Camp Fire Girls. Marian also loved to play doctor with her dolls and at one point even considered medicine as a career.

Over all, though, what Marian loved was singing. All three Anderson sisters sang in the junior choir in Union Baptist Church. Marian would sing the low parts (bass) as well as the high parts (soprano), but she felt most comfortable as a contralto, which is the lowest female singing part.

One day, the choir director, Alexander Robinson, gave a song to Marian and her playmate, Viola Johnson, to sing in the children's service. The two girls sang the duet so well that Robinson invited them back the next week to sing it in the main service.

Church members, friends, and family quickly recognized the singing talent of six-year-old Marian. Word of her outstanding singing spread throughout the African-American community. Her Aunt Mary Pritchard, who sang in the senior choir, began taking Marian to sing at various church and community affairs. Sometimes, Marian would earn close to a dollar at these events.

Once, while on an errand for her mother, Marian noticed a flyer lying in the street. When she picked it up, she saw that it featured her own picture and name with the words "Come hear the baby contralto." Marian was so excited by the flyer that when she reached home, she realized that she had bought potatoes instead of the bread she was sent to get. She returned to the store with the flyer still clutched in her hand.

As the young girl grew, so did her singing. From the pews, Anna and John Anderson listened with pride to their daughters in the choir. The poor but musically rich family shared many happy times together.

Then a tragedy struck the Andersons that tested their love and their faith. One day at work in 1910, Marian's father was accidentally injured by a blow to his head. Shortly after, John Anderson died. Marian was just thirteen years old.

▲ ▲ ▲

Her husband's death tossed Anna Anderson into widowhood with three young daughters to support. Some suggested that she place the girls in a home, like an orphanage. Anna Anderson, grounded in her strong religious faith, resolved to keep her family together. Marian Anderson later said of her mother, "She became a father to us as well as a mother and earned our whole livelihood by taking in washing. It was terribly difficult for her, I know."[7] Although

Anna Anderson had taught school in Virginia, she did not have a teaching license for Pennsylvania. To support the family, she took in laundry and eventually worked as a cleaning woman in the Wanamaker Department Store. She moved the family once again to live with her husband's parents on Fitzwater Street.

Grandmother Anderson was a large, authoritative woman who clearly ruled the Anderson household. Marian's aunt and two cousins lived in the house as well. Grandmother Anderson also watched other children whose mothers went to work. She had very strong opinions about raising children, including a rule that children should eat hot cereal, especially oatmeal, every morning for breakfast.

Grandfather Anderson, on the other hand, was a less imposing member of the household. Although he was African American, Grandfather Anderson was of the Jewish faith. He observed Saturdays as his Sabbath and taught Marian about the Passover holiday. This exposure to the Jewish faith would later enable her to feel comfortable forming relationships not only with Jewish people but with people of other faiths as well.

Through all Marian's difficulties—losing her father, adjusting to living in Grandmother Anderson's crowded home—singing remained a constant in her life. Now, at age thirteen, she began to sing in the senior choir as well as the junior choir. The director would give her the music to take home, and she would study all the parts. Because of her extraordinary range, from deep bass to high soprano, Marian could fill in for anyone in the choir, male or female.

Marian learned a great deal from singing in the choirs, but she also wanted to attend a music school for formal voice lessons. The members of her church recognized her need for more training and offered to pay the school fees. With high hopes, Marian eagerly set out to apply to a music school in Philadelphia. When she arrived there, though, she received a different kind of lesson.

Growing up in South Philadelphia, Marian and her sisters were friends with the white children, mostly Irish, who lived in their neighborhood. The children played in one another's houses with no awareness of racial differences. One white girl even stayed at the Anderson home until her father picked her up after work. However, when Marian went to apply to music school, the difference of being black, she said, hit her like a fist in the middle of her stomach.[8]

At the music school, Marian joined a line in front of the window where a young white girl was handing out the applications. Patiently, Marian waited her turn and even continued to wait after the girl passed her over to help the person behind her. Finally, everyone had received an application and had left except Marian. She later described what happened next:

> She spoke to me then, but in a different tone of voice. . . . "What do you want?" was what she said. I told her an application blank. . . . She raised her upper lip as if she smelled something bad and said to me, "We don't take colored."[9]

Deeply shocked and hurt by the girl's words, Marian hurried home to tell her mother what had happened.[10] Anna Anderson tried to comfort her daughter. She told her that the Lord would make another way. In her later years, Marian Anderson stated that her one regret was that she never had the opportunity to attend music school. Ironically, the music school that refused her eventually closed down, and Anderson went on to become an international performer.

At one of the gala concerts held at Union Baptist Church, Roland Hayes, a well-known African-American tenor, appeared as a guest soloist. Hayes was the first African-American classical singer to receive international fame. His tenor voice was called a voice of beauty. He toured extensively in the United States and abroad. In Europe, he sang in the major cities before audiences that included royalty. He was also the first African-American singer to perform with a major American orchestra. On the concert stage, Hayes popularized the religious songs known as Negro spirituals, which were created by slaves. The African-American author James Weldon Johnson described spirituals as a "body of songs voicing all the cardinal virtues of Christianity—patience, forbearance, love, faith, and hope—through a necessarily modified form of primitive African music."[11] Some of the well-known spirituals are "Swing Low, Sweet Chariot," "He's Got the Whole World in His Hands," "Sometimes I Feel Like a Motherless Child," and "Nobody Knows the Trouble I've Seen."

Hayes also sang German, Italian, and French classical songs. Hayes's artistry had a great influence on Marian Anderson. At one of his appearances, he sang a few of the foreign songs. Some of the church members grumbled that if "their Marian" had performed, at least they could have understood the words.[12] The choir director invited Marian to sing on the next program with Hayes. Aware that the Anderson family was short of funds, the congregation took up an extra collection for her, a total of $17.02. Anderson went shopping with her mother for a new dress, but they found the clothes too costly. Instead, they purchased some white material and gold trim, and they sewed a pretty dress for Marian.

Marian's singing impressed Roland Hayes so much that he paid a visit to her home to speak with her family. Hayes thought that Marian should study with his well-respected voice teacher, Arthur Hubbard, who lived in Boston. Hayes had arranged for Hubbard to accept her as a student without charge. Of course, Marian wanted to jump at the offer. But Grandmother Anderson opposed the idea. Grandmother Anderson thought that Marian, still a schoolgirl, was too young to leave home, and why did she need singing lessons when she was singing already?[13] Anna Anderson would not go against her mother-in-law's wishes. Therefore, the family's answer to Hayes's offer was no. He continued to help Marian anyway by referring her for engagements and including her in some of his concerts.

As Marian's mother often told her, another way would be found. In 1915, John Thomas Butler, a Philadelphia actor and family friend, took Marian to meet Mary Saunders Patterson, a well-known local African-American soprano. After hearing Marian sing, Patterson agreed to give her free vocal lessons. Patterson believed that a young singer should not begin a career in debt.

At last Marian would get the formal training she had wanted. When Patterson asked Marian how she produced a musical note, Marian just stared at her with a blank face. Now a high school student, Marian had been singing for a number of years, but this was her very first singing lesson. Marian explained to Patterson that she just opened her mouth, "and there it was with ease—a high B, or C, or a low D."[14]

For Marian, that spontaneous style of singing was about to come to an end. And the long journey of becoming a professional singer was just beginning.

Chapter 3

SINGING LESSONS

Throw your voice toward a corner of the ceiling, high up, where the two walls join, Mary Saunders Patterson told Anderson. It was the first time Anderson actually thought about singing. Until then, she had sung naturally, without much consideration. But as she tried to push the notes toward the corner of the room, she knew that this new, thoughtful way of singing would shape her into the professional that she wished to be. Anderson said that it was "excellent . . . to realize that the voice could be controlled and channeled."[1]

Patterson taught Anderson some songs by Franz Schubert, an Austrian composer who wrote the German art songs known as *lieder*. The lyrics of these songs are poems that express subtle emotions. *Lieder* are written for a solo voice with piano accompaniment. *Lieder* by Schubert became Anderson's favorite, particularly "Ave Maria."

Patterson also groomed Anderson as a professional in other ways. She gave Anderson a beautiful evening gown to wear for her performances. Anderson treasured the gown for years, even after she could afford to buy expensive gowns.

One day, Patterson asked Anderson whom she would like as an accompanist. The question thrilled Anderson.[2] She had begun to make money from her singing, and with some of it, she had taken piano lessons. Anderson had learned enough to accompany herself at recitals, but having her own accompanist signaled a major step up in her career. Patterson suggested William "Billy" King, a popular young musician who accompanied musical guests such as Roland Hayes when they visited Philadelphia.

At the time, Billy King was the accompanist for a young soprano, Lydia McClain. Anderson doubted that King would choose to work with her instead of McClain. As it turned out, Anderson and King were thrown together by circumstances beyond their control.

McClain, King, and Anderson were scheduled to perform at a church in Orange, New Jersey. The three traveled there on a train together, and a doctor friend of McClain's joined them. When the train reached their station, McClain and her friend stayed on. Expecting McClain to show up later, King and Anderson went on to the church. But McClain never showed up. She and the doctor had other plans—they eloped!

Still, the show went on. Anderson sang the entire program with King as her accompanist. From then on, King was her accompanist as well as her manager and friend. From his experiences of appearing with other performers, he was able to book many engagements for Anderson. They focused on African-American colleges such as Hampton Institute in Virginia and Howard University in Washington, D.C. The advantage of appearing there was that the colleges would then arrange for them to perform in local churches and theaters.

It was on her first trip south to one of these engagements that Anderson learned about some of the harsher aspects of African-American life in the early 1900s. In 1896, the United States Supreme Court had issued the *Plessy* v. *Ferguson* decision. The Court ruled that segregation could be practiced in the United States if the facilities were "separate but equal." As a result, most public service facilities were separated into "colored" and "white" sections: buses, trains, drinking fountains, even parking lots. Since hospitals and cemeteries were segregated also, it was said that people were segregated by laws from cradle to grave. The laws were called "Jim Crow laws," and when Anderson took her first trip to the South, she met the Jim Crow laws face-to-face. Fortunately, her mother was by her side.

Anderson had a singing engagement in Savannah, Georgia. To get there, she and her mother boarded an integrated train in Philadelphia. As the train approached Washington, D.C., a conductor announced, "Coming into Washington! Coming into Washington!"[3] At the Washington station, the black and white passengers were separated to comply with the "Jim Crow laws." Anderson and her mother moved with the other African Americans to the first coach of the train, called the Jim Crow car. When Anderson got there, she was shocked. The Jim Crow car was separate, but there was nothing equal about it. The train car was dirty, dark, and poorly ventilated. The travelers could not even open the windows because smoke and soot from the engine would blow in. Anderson and her mother could see that the grimy conditions affected the other African-American passengers as well. Anderson stated, "I had looked closely at my people in that train. Some seemed to be embarrassed to the core."[4]

Despite these obstacles, Anderson persevered with her singing and her education. She first attended William Penn High School, where she took business classes. She struggled with the shorthand and bookkeeping studies. In 1918, the principal, aware of her singing talent, suggested that she transfer to South Philadelphia High School for Girls, where she could pursue an academic education.

Dr. Lucy Wilson, the principal of South Philadelphia High School, took a special interest in the talented student. She allowed Anderson to skip classes for her singing engagements with King and to make up the schoolwork later. At Patterson's suggestion, Anderson had moved on to study with a new vocal teacher, Agnes Reifsnyder, who was a contralto like Anderson. Reifsnyder introduced Anderson to the songs of Johannes Brahms, a nineteenth-century German composer. In her lessons with Reifsnyder, Anderson concentrated on her breathing by doing special exercises. Reifsnyder also showed Anderson how to select and arrange songs for her recitals.

One day, Wilson arranged for Anderson to meet a famous vocal teacher, Giuseppe Boghetti, who had trained many well-known concert and opera singers. The audition took place at the end of a long hard day for Boghetti, whose schedule was already filled with students. He was abrupt with them and waited impatiently for Anderson to sing the spiritual "Deep River." Years later, Boghetti described her audition: "A tall calm girl poured out 'Deep River' in the twilight and made me cry."[5] Moved to tears by her singing, Boghetti immediately accepted Anderson as a student.

Anderson's usual problem arose: money. Once again, the members of Union Baptist Church came through. They formed the "Fund for Marian Anderson's Future." In May 1920, the church held a gala concert and raised about $600 for the lessons.

A tough taskmaster, Boghetti set out immediately to work on Anderson's musical scales. He told her that E flat was her best tone. To even out her unequal tones, he devised a vocal exercise starting from E flat and then moving up and down the scale. Anderson appreciated the laborious exercises. She still had not surrendered the spontaneous method of singing. Anderson stated that she learned under Boghetti that "there is no shortcut. You must understand the how and why of what you are doing."[6]

Boghetti introduced Anderson to songs by Robert Schumann, a German composer, and Hugo Wolf, an Austrian composer. He also helped her with her Italian and taught her Italian arias. An aria is an elaborate vocal solo set to music. Arias express a character's thoughts or feelings in an opera. Boghetti, a tenor, loved to sing opera, and he and Anderson would do operatic scenes together. Anderson enjoyed performing the scenes, but Boghetti discouraged her from pursuing opera as a career. He knew that opera was closed to African-American singers, a fact that Anderson would change many years later.

In 1923, Anderson entered a singing competition sponsored by the Philharmonic Society of Philadelphia. She won first prize and received a certificate. The local newspapers reported the results. Anderson's name appeared in the announcements, which noted that she was the first African American to take first prize.

Anderson and Billy King continued to perform in various cities. As Anderson began to appear in larger places, especially theaters, she felt as if she had a real singing career. And her fees began to reflect it, increasing to $50 an engagement. This was a good sum, but Anderson had to pay King and her other expenses out of it.

After one concert in Wilmington, Delaware, she was invited to a reception at the home of the Fishers, a prominent African-American family in the area. At the door of the Fishers' home, a tall, good-looking young man barred her with his arm from entering. The young man laughed at his joke, but it only annoyed Anderson. After teasing her, the young man let her pass. Anderson found out later that his name was Orpheus Hodges Fisher, nicknamed "King." Fisher, an art student, became her friend and later her suitor. Little did she know that the young man who barred her from his house would one day marry her and help build her a home.

Over time, Anderson's fees increased to about $300 per performance. She was able to cover her expenses and put money away into a savings account. One day, a house was put up for sale on South Martin Street, a few blocks away from Grandmother Anderson's. Although she appreciated her grandparents' generosity in taking her family in, Anderson wanted a place where she could live with her mother and sisters in a home of their own. Anderson decided to purchase the house. She used her savings for the down payment. Soon the deed was signed. The house needed renovations, and hardwood floors were installed. Finally, the day arrived for them to move in. Anderson recalled that they were "incredibly happy" to be in their own home.[7] When her sister Ethel got married, Ethel and her husband moved into the house next door, and eventually the two houses were joined. The family chose to live on that block long after Anderson became wealthy enough to move them into an affluent area.

As their performances grew more successful, Anderson and King began to appear before mixed, or integrated, audiences. Soon they were confident enough to schedule a recital in New York City. The date was set for April 23, 1924, in Town Hall. Boghetti assisted Anderson with the program, which included four German *lieder*. Following Boghetti's instructions, Anderson arrived early and practiced some vocal exercises. She felt special getting ready for her Town Hall debut. The feeling quickly vanished when she saw that only a few people showed up. Also, Anderson had difficulty with the German language, and the music critics noted that in their reviews.

Dejected, Anderson returned home. For a year, she avoided Boghetti and refused to sing. She even considered a career change to medicine. During this time, Anna Anderson continued to work at her cleaning job at the Wanamaker Department Store. One day, she woke up feeling ill. Anderson could see that the demanding and tiresome work had affected her elderly mother's health. Anna Anderson was in no shape to go to her cleaning job. The next morning, Anderson called Wanamaker's and told the supervisor that her mother would not be in to work that day or any day ever again. The desire to support her mother and her irrepressible love of singing motivated Anderson to resume her singing career. Of all her achievements, Marian Anderson has highlighted the moment she terminated her mother's laborious job as the happiest moment of her life.[8]

After the year had passed, Anderson returned to Boghetti for lessons. In 1925, she entered a competition sponsored by the National Music League in New York City. The prize was a chance to appear as a soloist with the New York Philharmonic Orchestra in Lewisohn Stadium in New York City.

Boghetti prepared Anderson for the contest and accompanied her to New York. As she entered the large auditorium, she saw the competitors seated downstairs and the judges seated upstairs in the balcony. Three hundred vocalists were waiting, so the judges wasted no time. When they had heard enough from a contestant, the judges used a noisy clicker to signal the singer to stop and exit the stage.

For the contest, Anderson chose to sing "O Mio Fernando," an aria from the Donizetti opera *La Favorita*. Boghetti told her not to stop even if she heard the clicker from upstairs. As she sang, she listened for the clicker from the balcony. It never came. The judges allowed Anderson to sing the whole song. When she came to the end, a burst of applause erupted from the other contestants in the auditorium. One judge asked her to sing another song. A few days later, Boghetti was notified that Anderson was chosen as one of the sixteen semifinalists. From those sixteen, the judges would choose four finalists. Anderson and Boghetti traveled back to New York for the semifinal competition. Before they could return to Philadelphia, a telephone call gave them the good news. There would be no finals. Anderson had won the contest.

The concert with the New York Philharmonic Orchestra took place on August 26, 1925, in Lewisohn Stadium. In a new light blue dress, Anderson took her place beside the conductor. She peered out at the packed stadium. Years of experience gave her the confidence to face the huge crowd. Among them sat her family with her ever-supportive mother. The program consisted of her prizewinning aria, "O Mio Fernando," and several spirituals. After the aria, the audience burst into applause. Even the string musicians showed their appreciation by tapping their bows on their music stands. A music reviewer later wrote of the concert, "A remarkable voice was heard last night at the Lewisohn Stadium. . . . She had given a recital at Town Hall on April 23, 1924, but that had hinted little at the astonishing vocal powers displayed by the young singer last night."[9] Obviously, Anderson's lessons had paid off. But she had more to learn.

Shortly after the concert, Anderson appeared in New York City's Carnegie Hall with a renowned African-American group, the Hall Johnson Choir. After the performance, Arthur Judson, the president of a concert management agency, introduced himself. He complimented her singing and suggested that she visit his office to discuss signing on with him. At Carnegie Hall, he mentioned a fee of $750 per performance, but when she visited his office (with Boghetti) he offered her only $500. The decrease in fee disappointed her.[10] But $500 was still a good sum. Also, an association with the Judson name would give her career a boost. Anderson accepted his offer.

The new management did secure higher fees for her, but the number of her engagements declined. Despite her successful appearance in Lewisohn Stadium, opportunities were still closed to Anderson because of her race. Some people even said, "A wonderful voice—it's too bad that she's a Negro."[11]

Judson told Anderson that he had a woman friend who was very knowledgeable about singing. This friend suspected that Anderson was really a soprano instead of a contralto. He wanted Anderson to meet with his friend to test her suspicions. Anderson knew that she was a contralto and that to sing outside her range could ruin her voice. Judson's uncertainty about something so essential to her career upset her.[12]

Judson also suggested that she study with Frank La Forge, a New York voice teacher with a reputation for working with famous singers. Anderson took this advice, even though it caused discord with Boghetti. He did not think she needed another teacher. Angry, Boghetti refused to share his student, but Anderson decided to study with La Forge anyway. (She returned to Boghetti later, after she left La Forge.)

Although Anderson's recital fees had grown beyond her expectations, she had difficulty paying for La Forge's costly singing lessons. She had other expenses and a mortgage to pay as well. Traveling from Philadelphia to New York also added to the cost of the lessons. La Forge proposed that she take his class before 9:00 A.M. At that early time, he would give her an hour of instruction for the price of a half hour. Eager for the lessons that could advance her career, Anderson did not mind rising at the crack of dawn to travel to his studio.

Anderson worked on her German songs with La Forge and could hear the improvement. Soon, though, even the half-hour rate became more than she could afford. She told La Forge that she would have to stop. Once again, someone came through for her: An anonymous scholarship paid for the lessons. Anderson suspected that the donor was La Forge's sister.[13]

Although her German improved, a recital in La Forge's studio showed Anderson that there was more work to be done. Once, while singing a *lied*, she forgot some of the words and had to improvise. The embarrassing incident haunted her.

Anderson seriously considered traveling to Europe to gain command of some foreign languages. Judson disagreed. He wanted her to stay and perform in the United States. He tried to discourage her by telling her that she would be going to Europe only to satisfy her ego.

Dissatisfied with her stagnant career, Anderson decided to go to Europe anyway.

Chapter 4

"MARIAN FEVER ABROAD"

In 1927, Anderson sailed on the *Ile de France* for England. After discussing the trip with her family—as usual, they were very supportive—she purchased a second-class ticket with her savings. As friends and family waved good-bye, she boarded the ship with high expectations. Billy King had contacted Roger Quilter, a friend in London, to help her get settled after she arrived. Alone on the ship, though, she felt homesick and lonely.[1] One evening, while on the deck, a gentleman spoke to her in French. Anderson decided to try her high school French on her fellow traveler. She responded with a cheerful comment about *le soleil*—meaning the moon. The gentleman's amused reaction alerted her to her mistake: *Le soleil* meant the sun. Quickly, she retreated to her cabin. Still, the anticipation of studying abroad kept her spirits afloat. The exciting adventure even hastened the long journey.

When Anderson reached the London train station, she immediately telephoned Quilter. Instead of a helpful message, though, she received some bad news. Quilter had become ill and was hospitalized. The news proved to be an omen for the trip. Loaded down with bags, stranded in a strange city, Anderson wondered what to do. Fortunately, she remembered a family friend, John Payne, who lived in London. On a visit to Philadelphia, Payne had extended an open invitation to her family to stay with him if they ever visited London.

Anderson telephoned Payne, and he extended the same friendly invitation. She solved one problem only to discover another one. She realized that she had lost her music case, which held not only her music but also her traveler's checks totaling $1,500. Agonized, Anderson returned to the train station with Payne. They searched the platforms for the case. Finally, a police officer suggested that they check the lost-and-found department. There they found the music case with everything intact, including the checks.[2]

After a short stay in London, Anderson visited a small town in nearby Sussex to study with Raimund von Zur Mühlen, a famous vocal teacher. Master, as he was known, was an expert on *lieder*. Anderson was thrilled to meet the elderly man who sat in a chair with his cane at his side. Master asked her to sing. When she finished the *lied* "Im Abendrot," he asked if she knew what she had sung. Anderson answered that she was ashamed to admit that she did not know what it meant.[3]

Master told her that if she did not know the meaning of the words, she should not sing them. He lent her a book of Schubert songs to study. At the time, Anderson was staying at the home of a couple named Newburg. Mr. Newburg, who knew German, helped Anderson with the verses. Anderson met only sporadically with Master because he had become ill, but she learned a lot from him. Unfortunately, Master was soon unable to teach at all.

Quilter returned home from the hospital, and Anderson often visited his house. A patron of the arts, Quilter opened his home to many musicians. He even arranged a recital for Anderson at Wigmore Hall in London. Over all, despite the support from her new friends, her trip to Europe failed to bring the desired results, and she left disappointed. She had not achieved her goal of becoming an expert singer of *lieder*.[4]

Anderson returned home to friends and family, whom she had missed very much. One special friend was Orpheus "King" Fisher, the young man she had met in Delaware. Fisher had visited her in Philadelphia, and eventually he became her boyfriend. When Anderson returned from England, though, another male friend met her at the boat. Fisher heard of it and was distant and aloof when he next visited her.

Anderson was not home long when she felt once again that her career was at a standstill. She resolved to go back to Europe, this time to Germany, where she could work on *lieder*. She did not know where the money would come from, but she believed what her mother often said: A way would be found.

At a Chicago concert sponsored by the Alpha Kappa Alpha sorority, two men approached Anderson. They represented the Julius Rosenwald Fund, a foundation that gave education fellowships to African Americans. They asked about her career goals, and Anderson told them of her desire to go to Germany. She filled out a fellowship application. Anderson requested a half-year fellowship because she had some already-scheduled engagements to fulfill. Heartened that a way had been found, Anderson packed her trunk and was set to sail when she was informed that the fellowship was for a whole year. Immediately, she explained her predicament. The

Rosenwald Fund agreed to make an exception, and Anderson sailed for Europe for a half-year stay.

In Berlin, Germany, Anderson rented a room from the von Edburgs, a couple who spoke only German. It was difficult at first, but Anderson was there to learn the language. The husband coached Anderson in German. She became more at ease with the German songs, but the *lieder* still had to be mastered. Anderson began to study with a German vocal coach, Michael Raucheisen. One day, as they worked in his studio, two men joined them. They introduced themselves as Rule Rasmussen, a Norwegian manager, and Kosti Vehanen, a pianist from Finland. They had heard of a performance Anderson gave in Berlin.

A concert manager in Scandinavian countries, Helmer Enwall, sent the men to see about a possible Anderson concert in Sweden. Anderson was a very common name in Sweden, and Enwall thought that an African-American singer named Anderson would be a successful act there. Anderson was scheduled to give a small recital, and the men went to hear her. She sang a few operatic arias and a number of spirituals. Although they were unaccustomed to the spirituals, they were impressed with her voice. As they left the concert, Vehanen told Rasmussen that if Anderson succeeded in using the extraordinary range of her voice, she would become a marvelous singer.[5]

Helmer Enwall arranged for Anderson to appear in six recitals in Scandinavia: two each in Oslo, Norway; Stockholm, Sweden; and Helsinki, Finland. Each appearance depended on the success of the previous one. In Oslo, the first concert was enthusiastically received. The audience continued to applaud, even into the intermission. As a result, the second performance quickly sold out. Many English-speaking Norwegians called Anderson at her hotel to talk about music or the United States. They also made special song requests. Some even brought her flowers.

In Stockholm, the Swedish people seemed less enthusiastic. Although Enwall assured her that the first concert went well, Anderson was not convinced. However, her second concert drew a larger audience.

The Helsinki audiences received her as warmly as the Oslo audiences had. Since her accompanist, Kosti Vehanen, was from Finland, he also helped to make her feel comfortable in his homeland.

Those first six concerts multiplied into many more over the subsequent months. Anderson performed in Copenhagen, Denmark, and English-speaking admirers there readily and graciously welcomed her. Anderson felt accepted as an individual there. One Danish reporter wrote that the Danes were not conscious of her dark color. When she walked onto the stage, he wrote, they noticed first her gracious appearance and then were captivated by her refined art. An American reporter wrote of her Copenhagen performance that Anderson, dressed in a black velvet gown with orchids at her waist, caused an overflow of emotion with her exceptional singing.[6]

In the Scandinavian countries, Anderson felt that people judged her solely for her qualities as a human being and as an artist. Their acceptance freed her to take risks with her singing. Anderson felt her ambitions were possible.[7] Also, while she was in Europe, she received a long letter from her friend King Fisher. Things were definitely going well this time around. The six months quickly passed, and Anderson had to return home.

One day, Anderson received a surprising telegram from Enwall, asking her to come back to Europe with a promise of twenty concerts. Soon another telegram arrived offering forty concerts. And then another one followed offering sixty concerts. Anderson trusted Enwall to fulfill his promise of concerts. She applied to the Rosenwald Fund for the second half of the fellowship and received the money. In 1933, Anderson journeyed back to Europe and stayed there for two years.

Enwall more than delivered on his promise. Over the next twelve months, Anderson gave more than one hundred concerts throughout Scandinavia. The audiences embraced her with as much enthusiasm as before. Even the Swedes demonstrated their appreciation openly during this second tour. Some wrote her letters explaining their earlier reluctance. Photographs and articles appeared in the newspapers. One article even characterized the sensation as "Marian Fever."[8]

When Vehanen became Anderson's accompanist, he suggested that she study some Scandinavian songs, especially songs by Jean Sibelius. This great Finnish composer was highly revered in his country. One evening, Vehanen took Anderson to meet Sibelius at his villa. Sibelius warmly welcomed them into his home. He offered them coffee, but Vehanen thought that Anderson should first sing the Sibelius song she had prepared. As her coach, Vehanen was nervous for her, but Anderson sang in her usual self-assured manner. When she finished the song, Sibelius called out not for coffee but for champagne. With a toast of champagne, Sibelius told her that his roof was too low for her voice.[9] Later, Sibelius dedicated his song "Solitude" to her.

Coincidentally, Sol Hurok was in Europe during this time. Hurok was one of the most powerful and influential impresarios of his time. He was the manager for some of the great artists in the world. One evening, while strolling along a street in Paris, he noticed an announcement for a concert given by an American contralto. He told his wife that he would just take a look at the singer. In the Paris hall, filled to capacity, Hurok saw Anderson take her place near the piano and begin to sing. Unprepared for her exceptional voice, Hurok stated, "Chills danced up my spine and my palms were wet. . . . Anyone who had ears to hear her then could hear the great future already present."[10]

Hurok invited her to a meeting. Excited, Vehanen and Anderson went to Hurok's office the next day. Anderson was aware of his reputation as a daring manager. Earlier in her career, she had tried unsuccessfully to meet with him.

At the meeting, Hurok told her that he wanted to represent Anderson in her own country. He offered her a contract for fifteen concerts. Since she had been working with the Arthur Judson agency, Anderson spoke with the management there first. They could not guarantee her the same number of concerts, so they released her from her agreement with the agency. Anderson signed a contract with Hurok for fifteen concerts. These were just the beginning of many more to come.

Anderson was not quite ready to return to the United States. She still had some concerts scheduled in Austria and Brussels, and what a boost to her career they proved to be!

Chapter 5

ONCE IN A HUNDRED YEARS

Vienna, Austria, the home of the famous composers Ludwig von Beethoven, Johannes Brahms, and Franz Schubert, held a special event for Anderson. The concert took place in a large building that held several small concert halls and a larger Great Hall for major events. When Anderson walked onto one of the smaller concert stages, a sparsely seated audience greeted her. The poor attendance bothered her, but being a professional, she sang her very best anyway. Intermission came, and Anderson took her break. When she returned to the stage, a strange sight surprised her. The concert hall was full of people. Apparently, during the intermission Anderson's audience spoke so excitedly about her performance that the audience of the Great Hall concert decided to switch over to Anderson's concert. And not only did the audience enlarge in size, but the experience grew in emotion as well. After she sang Bach's "Komm' süsser Tod," Anderson noticed people wiping tears from their eyes.[1]

In Salzburg, Anderson reached an even greater milestone in her career. The city, known for its music festivals, attracted famous artists from all over the world. In the summer of 1935, Anderson's artistry still was not well known, although her concerts had been enthusiastically received. An American woman, Gertrude Moulton, wanted to give Anderson the proper attention, so she arranged a private recital for about four hundred people in the Hôtel de l'Europe. Many famous musical artists and music lovers sat in the audience that included an archbishop and another celebrity, Arturo Toscanini. Toscanini was one of the world's greatest conductors of his time.

Anderson sang her best for this impressive audience. A writer, Vincent Sheean, described what happened: "She sang Bach, Schubert, and Schumann, with a final group of Negro spirituals. Her superb voice commanded the closest attention of that audience from its first note."[2] The archbishop even requested an encore of "Ave Maria."

After the concert, many went backstage to express their admiration and appreciation to Anderson. Toscanini also visited her backstage. Overwhelmed by the presence of the great artist, Anderson did not hear what he had to say. A friend nearby reported that Toscanini told her, "Yours is a voice, one hears once in a hundred years." Vehanen was also present, and he remembered that Toscanini said, "What I heard today one is privileged to hear only in a hundred years."[3] The "what" meant not just her voice but her whole artistry, the result of years of study and hard work.

When the time came to return to the United States, Anderson faced a unique problem. Should she return with Vehanen as her accompanist? The question arose not because of his musicianship but because of his race. As a white man, Vehanen could cause much difficulty for her. First, many white people, especially in the South, would strongly oppose Anderson's having him as her accompanist. In addition, many black people might view it as a sort of betrayal. Had Anderson become too famous to appear with a member of her own race? they might ask. Anderson pondered the dilemma. Vehanen reminded her that the art always came first for her. Anderson then informed her manager that she and Vehanen would arrive in New York on December 17, 1935.

Her first major concert, staged at New York's Town Hall, was a huge success, despite her injured leg in a cast. She was finally recognized as an accomplished artist in her own country. Anderson appeared in various cities across the United States. In March 1936, a reviewer wrote of a concert in Carnegie Hall in New York, "A capacity house and boundless enthusiasm testified last evening to the popularity achieved here by Miss Marian Anderson."[4]

Shortly after, Anderson and Vehanen returned to Europe. Her popularity had spread across the continent and beyond. Once, a request even came for her to sing in Germany, which was at that time ruled by the anti-Semitic and racist dictator Adolf Hitler. When it could not be affirmed that Anderson was 100 percent white, the offer was abruptly withdrawn.

Anderson and Vehanen toured the Soviet Union several times. On each occasion, the people there embraced her performances. On their arrival in the city of Leningrad (now St. Petersburg), an English-speaking woman asked for the text of the scheduled songs in order to translate them into Russian. Anderson gave her the songs, including several spirituals. Anderson had been warned about singing spirituals because religious observance was outlawed in the Soviet Union. Before Anderson sang each song, the woman explained the meaning of the words. Vehanen stated that "the management changed the titles and gave them a less religious tone if they were of a spiritual nature: For example, instead of saying 'Ave Maria' by Schubert, they would say 'an aria by Schubert.'" Religious or not, the people applauded each song and demanded encores. And to make sure they got what they wanted, they shouted, "Ave Maria," and not "the aria by Schubert."[5]

Several important experiences marked the tours of the Soviet Union. In Leningrad, Anderson dined with another world-famous performer, the African-American bass-baritone Paul Robeson. In Moscow, Anderson gave several recitals in the large hall of the Conservatory. This hall had a government box on the right side of the stage. As was customary, waiters would pass through the artists' room backstage to take refreshments to the government box during intermission. At one recital, though, Anderson and Vehanen noticed that things were strikingly different. The whole hall was dark. A large spotlight was thrown on Anderson. The audience could see only the performers and the piano. When Anderson and Vehanen asked about the strong light and dark hall, their Soviet companion sounded frightened and said that he did not know. During intermission, they also noticed that the waiters passed through with large trays of appetizing fruits and pastries. After the concert, no one would reveal who was in the government box. It was later rumored that it was the Soviet dictator Joseph Stalin.[6]

In Moscow, the great theater director Konstantin Stanislavsky gave a tea for Anderson at his apartment. At the tea, he surprised her with a proposal: Would she like to stay in Moscow and study the role of Carmen in the opera by Georges Bizet? The offer greatly interested her, but other singing commitments prevented her from accepting it. On leaving Moscow, Stanislavsky sent her a bouquet of white lilacs. Shortly after, Stanislavsky died. Later in her career, Anderson regretted not accepting his offer. She recalled, "How important it is to take an opportunity when it comes."[7]

In 1938, Anderson and Vehanen set sail for South America on the SS *Augustus*. The ship stopped over in Dakar, the capital of French West Africa (Senegal today). Vehanen described Anderson as "happy as her feet touched African soil. . . . for her it was like coming home actually to be in the land where her forefathers had lived."[8]

After the ship left Africa, it headed to South America. Anderson gave a recital onboard for the seamen. In South America, her success continued. Vehanen had appraised the public in Buenos Aires as having superb musical taste. Anderson's audiences there responded with enthusiasm, and her concerts included a recital in the largest theater, where every seat was taken.

In Montevideo, the capital of Uruguay, a popular conductor failed to show up to conduct the orchestra for her. Instead, Vehanen would have to accompany Anderson on the piano. The situation was explained to the ticket holders, and they were offered refunds. Three tickets were returned. But thirty more were sold.[9]

Back home in the United States, Anderson's accomplishments caught the attention of many people, including President Franklin Delano Roosevelt. In 1936, he invited her to perform at the White House.

In 1938, Howard University bestowed on Anderson an honorary Ph.D. degree in music. A college may grant a person an honorary degree if the person demonstrates excellence in a particular field.

Many more honorary degrees for Anderson would follow over the years.

In January 1939, the National Association for the Advancement of Colored People (NAACP) announced that she would receive its prestigious Spingarn Medal, an award given annually to recognize the high achievement of an African American. The award was scheduled to be presented in July 1939. In the few months before the ceremony, an incident occurred that shook the nation.

Chapter 6

AN EASTER SUNDAY CONCERT

B y 1939, Anderson had performed to high acclaim in cities all over the world—London, Paris, Moscow, Buenos Aires, New York. Sol Hurok, in conjunction with Howard University, understandably thought that the time had come for a major performance in the capital of her own country. What should have been a routine request to reserve Constitution Hall in Washington, D.C., evolved into an event that challenged the very ideals and laws of the United States.

The music department of Howard University applied to Fred E. Hand, the manager of Constitution Hall, to reserve the hall for April 9, 1939, for Anderson's concert. Hand replied that a clause in the rental contract prohibited the presentation of Negro artists.[1] Sol Hurok asked if the hall would waive the restriction, and Hand replied that the hall was unavailable for April 9, 1939. Hurok then arranged for a white artist friend to request the available dates. The management informed his friend that April 8 and April 10 were open. Immediately, Hurok wired Hand and requested those dates.

Hand's reply was curt and to the point: "The hall is not available for a concert by Miss Anderson."[2]

Constitution Hall was owned, tax free, by the Daughters of the American Revolution (DAR), an organization of women with white ancestors who had served in the American Revolutionary War. When news spread of the ban on an appearance by Marian Anderson, telegrams and phone calls of protest flooded the DAR office. A group of musicians and clergy sent a telegram stating:

> We read with astonishment the reports in the press that the Daughters of the American Revolution have refused the use of Constitution Hall to Marian Anderson. . . . [It] places your organization . . . in the camp of those who today seek to destroy democracy, justice and liberty.[3]

At this same time, another controversy was brewing in Washington, D.C. Following the ban by the DAR, Howard University requested use of the Central High School auditorium for the concert. The superintendent of schools refused the request. The District of Columbia had a segregated school system of separate black and white schools. Because Central High School was a white school, the Board of Education refused to grant a permit for Anderson to appear there. In response, a Marian Anderson Protest Committee sprang up. The group gathered more than five thousand signatures for a petition against the school board's decision.

News articles and editorials decried the treatment of Anderson. Many of the comments compared the DAR and the school board to Adolf Hitler, the Nazi dictator of Germany.

Then, one protest rang out the loudest of them all across the nation. On February 27, 1939, the DAR received a resignation in protest from its most prominent member—First Lady Eleanor Roosevelt. In her "My Day" column, published in New York's *World-Telegram*, she wrote: "I belong to an organization in which I can do no active work. They have taken an action which has been widely talked of in the press. To remain as a member implies approval of that action, and therefore I am resigning."[4]

The story made the national headlines. Although Mrs. Roosevelt did not name the organization, it was clearly understood that she had resigned from the Daughters of the American Revolution.

Protests continued to pour in, including one from the mayor of New York, Fiorello La Guardia. The famous violinist Jascha Heifitz performed in Constitution Hall and afterward stated to the press that he was ashamed to play in an auditorium from which Anderson was barred. Other resignations flowed into the DAR office, including one from Mrs. Giuseppe Boghetti, the wife of Anderson's former voice teacher.

Although many opposed the DAR's ban, many others supported it. DAR president Mrs. Henry M. Roberts, Jr., received a standing ovation from DAR members when she presented the organization's defense. Roberts explained that the DAR had had unpleasant experiences when it went against the customs of the District of Columbia.[5] The customs that Roberts was referring to were the segregation policies practiced in Washington, D.C., at the time.

Sol Hurok was not upset by the controversy. He saw the ban as an opportunity to enlighten the public on what had been happening over the years. Hurok saw the furor as a culmination of the many injustices Anderson had endured in her career. He stated: "After the constantly recurring offenses . . . it was almost a relief when the

Daughters of the American Revolution presented Marian's friends with an issue big enough to bring out into the open."[6]

Hurok announced that Anderson would sing in a free open-air concert in the nation's capital. Hurok's press agent, Gerald Goode, and Walter White of the NAACP sought permission from the Department of the Interior, which had authority over the capital's parks. Secretary of the Interior Harold Ickes quickly granted permission, at the urging of Mrs. Roosevelt. It was settled. Marian Anderson would sing on the steps of the Lincoln Memorial on Easter Sunday, April 9, 1939.

One voice remained silent throughout the national uproar over this controversy. Anderson and her accompanist, Vehanen, on tour out west, rode without speaking as their train rolled by the California mountains. Before them lay newspapers with the disturbing news about the concert. As was his custom, Hurok had shielded Anderson from the ruckus surrounding the DAR ban. So she was as surprised by the reports as everyone else. In San Francisco, while passing a newsstand, Anderson had noticed the headline stating that Mrs. Roosevelt had taken a stand on the issue. Until then, she had not known that the incident had reached White House proportions. When she learned of Mrs. Roosevelt's resignation from the DAR, Anderson said, "What a wonderful woman she is! She not only knows what is right, but she also does the right thing."[7]

On the train, Anderson and Vehanen did not discuss the furor swirling around them. Newspaper reporters tried to shatter her silence with a barrage of questions wherever she went, but Anderson's response was brief: "I don't know any more about this than you."[8]

The day of the Lincoln Memorial concert was quickly approaching, and Anderson was undecided about going through with it. For a concert of hers to be such a sensational and political event was wholly contrary to her beliefs. Anderson believed that art should not be used for political purposes. The artistry itself should speak for the equality of the races. Still, Anderson realized that the whole incident had become something much bigger than just her singing in a concert hall. She later stated, "I could see that my significance as an individual was small in this affair. I had become, whether I liked it or not, a symbol, representing my people."[9] When the day arrived, her professionalism took over, and she was ready to take her place in the national spotlight.

On Easter Sunday, April 9, 1939, a brisk wind swirled around the more than seventy-five thousand people, black and white, who gathered at the foot of the Lincoln Memorial to hear the great contralto. A huge platform had been constructed for the public officials. Among the notable guests were Associate Justice Hugo L. Black of the Supreme Court; Secretary of the Treasury Henry Morgenthau; Dr. Mordecai W. Johnson, president of Howard University; social activist Mary Church Terrell; and members of Congress. And, of course, also present were Anderson's two sisters and her mother, Anna Anderson.

Secretary of the Interior Harold Ickes introduced Anderson to the crowd, which stretched from the monument, along the banks of the reflecting pool, to the mound of the Washington Monument. Also listening to his words were millions of people all over the nation with their ears glued to the latest means of communication— the radio. In his speech, Ickes declared, "In this great auditorium under the sky, all of us are free. When God gave us this wonderful outdoors and the sun, the moon, and the stars, He made no distinction of race, or creed, or color." He further stated, "Genius draws no color line. She had endowed Marian Anderson with such a voice as lifts any individual above his fellows, as is a matter of exultant pride to any race."[10]

Then, before the huge crowd charged with anticipation, Anderson appeared between the towering marble columns. Dressed in a long black velvet dress and mink coat around her shoulders, she strode toward the cluster of microphones. Before the breathtaking view of the mass of humanity, Anderson began. "America" was first. Among the other selections were "O Mio Fernando," "Ave Maria," and the spiritual "My Soul Is Anchored in the Lord." Each song received a burst of applause. She sang her final number, the spiritual "Nobody Knows the Trouble I've Seen," in her usual posture, with her eyes closed and hands clasped. The spiritual ended to thunderous applause.

Overwhelmed by the enormous support shown to her that day, Anderson told the crowd, "I can't tell you what you have done for me today. I thank you from the bottom of my heart again and again."[11]

The DAR incident and its aftermath had far-reaching effects beyond that Easter Sunday. The concert established a new way of protest in two ways. First, the concert permanently associated the image of Lincoln with the theme of racial equality. Second, the concert established a style of protest that included patriotic and spiritual music, prominent platform guests, and the Lincoln Memorial as a demonstration site.[12]

Marian Anderson and the Lincoln Memorial concert had a strong influence on a young African-American minister by the name of Martin Luther King, Jr. King often mentioned Anderson in his sermons. He referred to her singing of the spirituals, her devotion to her mother, and her upward struggle from a poor background.[13]

In June 1939, King George VI and Queen Elizabeth of England visited President and Mrs. Roosevelt. Anderson was one of the performers invited to entertain the royal couple. Despite the Lincoln Memorial concert, many people in Washington, D.C., still held on to their racist views. At a dinner held not long before Anderson was to sing at the White House, a woman asked Vehanen if he was ashamed of traveling with a black person. Vehanen responded that the woman could not even go to some of the places that welcomed Marian Anderson. Vehanen was indignantly challenged to name one such place. The doors of the White House, he replied, were open to welcome Anderson when the queen and king of England arrived but they would be closed to the woman.[14]

In July 1939, the NAACP awarded Anderson the Spingarn Medal. Anderson was further honored by having First Lady Eleanor Roosevelt present the award. Mrs. Roosevelt told the NAACP conference that Anderson had had the courage to meet many difficulties. In accepting the award, Anderson stated that she appreciated its significance and felt it was an honor to have received it from the first lady.[15]

In 1940, Vehanen returned to his home in Finland. Franz Rupp, a German pianist, replaced him as Anderson's accompanist. Rupp, who was Jewish, had fled his country when Hitler came to power. Rupp was an expert on German *lieder* and was well versed in the songs of Schubert. He taught Anderson a deeper understanding of the songs, and she gladly accepted his criticism. She even relearned some of the songs to improve her performance.

In Philadelphia, the Bok Award was given annually to an outstanding citizen of Philadelphia. The Bok Award had never been given to an African American, so Anderson never expected such an honor. Ironically, the only woman who had so far received the award was Dr. Lucy Wilson, Anderson's high school principal. In 1941, Anderson was named as the recipient of the award and its cash prize of $10,000, a huge sum at the time. Grateful for having been given so much assistance during her own career, Anderson used the money to establish the Marian Anderson Scholarship Award for young singers of all races.

In 1943, U.S. Secretary of the Interior Harold Ickes commissioned a mural commemorating the Easter Sunday concert. The mural, depicting the concert, decorates the lobby of the Department of the Interior.

That same year, another major event would take place in Anderson's life. This one would be very private and personal.

Chapter 7

MARRIED LIFE

T he secret is out . . . at long last!"[1] Those words appeared in a newspaper article in November 1943. The secret? Marian Anderson and Orpheus "King" Fisher had finally married! After a twenty-year friendship, the couple had married secretly at a private ceremony in Bethel, Connecticut, on July 17, 1943. Although Fisher had vigorously pursued Anderson's hand in marriage, she had delayed getting married to concentrate on her career.

Unlike Anderson, with her humble background, Fisher was a member of a prominent African-American family in Delaware. He had seven siblings, who worked in professions such as chemist, veterinarian, and Episcopal priest.[2] Fisher himself was an architect. For a black man, positions in architecture were difficult to obtain. Since he was light-skinned, he even once passed for white to secure a position in an architectural firm. Fisher worked for large architectural companies in Philadelphia and New York. Some of the buildings he helped design were the Empire State Building and Rockefeller Center in New York City.[3]

When the couple decided to marry, they began to search for a house. The same racial problems that affected their professional lives plagued their personal lives as well. After surveying a few houses, Fisher found an ideal house for them in Briarcliff Manor, a suburb north of New York City. The next week Anderson went to see it. When the agent saw the bride-to-be, he told Fisher that he would have to charge them $1,000 more. Apparently, the agent had mistaken Fisher for a white man. The couple offered to pay more, even $8,000 more. Finally, the agent told them that he could not sell them the house because of their race.[4]

During their search, the couple was also told that one resident did not want Anderson to live nearby because, as a musician, she would bring a certain well-known "Negro band leader" to the house for noisy all-night jazz sessions. Anderson did not even know the bandleader, and she was not a jazz singer.[5]

The couple decided that Fisher would purchase a house alone, and then they would marry. Fisher bought an old farmhouse and one hundred acres of land in Danbury, Connecticut. They bought that much acreage to avoid conflict with their neighbors.[6] After they married, they moved into their new home, but not without trouble. Sometimes to show racial hatred, people burn a cross on someone's property. This is a common practice of the hate group the Ku Klux Klan. A cross was burned on the Fishers' lawn, and they also received threatening mail. Fisher told an interviewer about these occurrences, although Anderson preferred not to give publicity to such things.[7]

After a few years, they sold the farmhouse and built a modern L-shaped house on the other side of the property. Fisher used his architectural skills to design the house just the way they wanted it. He also built a music studio for Anderson. For the first time, she could rehearse without worrying about disturbing others in the house. They named the estate Marianna Farm, after Anderson and her mother. It was a real farm with horses, sheep, chickens, and cows. Anderson sent fresh eggs and vegetables from the farm to her family in Philadelphia. She and Fisher especially liked to go horseback riding on their land.

Anderson also enjoyed sewing and upholstery. While touring, she often took a sewing machine with her. Once she took material to make slipcovers for furniture in her home. Fisher bet her that she would not finish them, but she did.

The amount of time Anderson spent on her singing tours complicated their life together. Fisher explained, "I don't like them [tours] but I know it's her career. I'm always very nervous when one is approaching because I don't like to see her go." He said that being married to Anderson was "like being married to an angel."[8]

Touring was a hardship for Anderson as well. She traveled with a record player, a typewriter, an iron, cameras, a sewing machine, cooking utensils, and up to twenty bags to hold her large wardrobe. Aware that a singer's appearance was just as important as her performance, Anderson paid close attention to her wardrobe. After she became successful, she wore gowns by famous designers such as Chanel. Tall as a model and with a fine figure, she wore the gowns with grace. One was of black lace embroidered with black pearls. Her elegance caused the southern reporters to call her beautiful, a description that was not normally used for African Americans at that time. They also referred to her as "Singer Anderson" or "Marian Anderson." In the South, African Americans were usually addressed by their first names regardless of their age. But Anderson's accomplishments caused the reporters to break from that tradition, although they still would not call her *Miss* Anderson.[9]

Anderson toured with Franz Rupp, her accompanist, and Isaac Joffe, her road manager from Hurok's office. The three got along well and enjoyed some lively games of cards on their long rides together. Still, the two white men were often accepted into places where Anderson was not. Sometimes she used the cooking utensils to prepare meals in her hotel rooms. The few hotels that would allow Anderson to book a room would request that she take her meals in her room. They also requested that she use the freight elevator instead of the elevator used by the other hotel guests. Often, to avoid these indignities, Anderson would stay as a guest in private homes.

In an interview, Anderson once discussed some of the experiences the three of them had had over the years touring together. One incident began with their hostess, a white woman, picking them up at the train station. She addressed Rupp and Joffe as *Mr.* Rupp and *Mr.* Joffe, but she addressed Anderson as *Marian*. As they passed through a poor African-American community, the woman told Anderson, "Marian, your people just love it here."[10] She then told Joffe, "Mr. Joffe, I was just telling Marian how much better off the 'Nigrahs' are down here where we love them and take care of them."[11] After dropping off Anderson at a private home, the woman drove Rupp and Joffe to a hotel. They were allowed to stay there, but Anderson was not.

The next day, when Anderson arrived at the auditorium for rehearsal, she noticed that Rupp and Joffe appeared very agitated about something. Later, at the concert, the two men seemed unusually nervous about the performance. Anderson wondered why, but she had to focus her attention on the concert. The first part of the performance ended to overwhelming applause. Anderson and Rupp left the stage to return holding hands for another bow, as was their usual routine. Anderson described the moment: "As we emerged from the wings, his hand in mine, you could have heard the well-known pin drop. Then there was an avalanche of sound, applause so much greater even than it had been before that it was like a roar over the whole auditorium."[12]

When the well-received concert ended, Anderson asked the two men about their earlier nervousness. They explained that the hostess had told them that if Anderson was seen onstage holding the hand of a white man, the hostess would not be responsible for what might be done to them.[13] As it turned out, her worry was unfounded. The audience responded with even more enthusiasm.

Another incident did not go as well. The three of them arrived by train for a concert and were greeted by a big welcoming committee. Anderson was presented with flowers, and photographers took pictures for the local newspapers. When they left the platform and started to go through the station to their waiting cars, a man blocked the waiting room door. He told them that Anderson could not pass through the "white" waiting room. She would have to use the "colored" waiting room. Rupp and Joffe started to protest, but Anderson stopped them. Not wanting to cause a scene, Anderson walked through the "colored" waiting room. The others in the group—Rupp, Joffe, the photographers, and members of the welcome committee—went through the "white" waiting room and waited for her by the cars.

Anderson began to use her success to try to change what the government could not or would not do. In her performance contracts, she added a clause that required "vertical segregation" in the seating arrangements. In the South, all the theaters were segregated, with black people sitting in the balcony, and white people sitting below in the orchestra seats. Anderson's clause required vertical separation: That is, sections of the balcony as well as the orchestra were reserved for each race. When she appeared before such audiences, Anderson always made it a point to bow first to the people seated in the black section.

As time passed, Anderson refused to appear before segregated audiences at all. It was the custom for white people to be sold concert tickets first. As Anderson became more famous, the block of tickets left over for black patrons got smaller and smaller. Anderson requested that the tickets be sold on a first-come, first-served basis, with equal choice of seat location. If the sponsors would not comply, she refused to perform. The refusal caused her to lose some engagements. It also produced threats of violence.

At a concert in Miami, Florida, sixty plainclothes detectives, including some from the Federal Bureau of Investigation, were brought in to prevent any incidents of violence. The sponsors of the concert had informed the white patrons that seats would be sold on a nonsegregated basis as was stated in Anderson's contract. In response, some whites bought whole rows of seats so they would not be sold to blacks. The sponsors were prepared for trouble, but the concert went on without incident.[14]

In 1941, the United States had entered World War II. Everyone joined the war effort. Some enlisted in the armed services, and some worked in factories. Like other performers, Anderson entertained the troops and participated in rallies to sell war bonds.

Anderson was invited to christen a new warship, the *Booker T. Washington*, named after the great African-American educator. She also christened a submarine, the *George Washington Carver*, named after the African-American agricultural chemist.

She continued to receive many awards. In 1943, she was honored by the government of Liberia, a West African country founded as a haven for freed American slaves. Liberia bestowed on her its highest honor, the Liberian Order of African Redemption.

In 1946, the government of Finland gave her its distinguished award, the Order of the White Rose. In 1952, she received from the king of Sweden the Litteris et Artibus medal, an award for outstanding achievement given annually to artists and scientists. Also in 1952, Anderson made her television debut on *The Ed Sullivan Show*. Anderson had performed regularly over the radio on the *Telephone Hour*.

Over the years, Anderson also had made recordings of the spirituals and classical songs of her repertoire. She recorded on labels such as RCA Victor. By 1956, her recording of Schubert's "Ave Maria" had sold more than 750,000 copies, and her albums had sold more than 250,000 copies.

Yet, despite her many achievements, there remained one unfulfilled dream: to sing in an opera. The dream eluded Anderson for many years—but not forever.

Chapter 8

A DREAM COMES TRUE

I n September 1954, Sol Hurok threw a party to celebrate the opening of a special production at the Metropolitan Opera House in New York City. The Metropolitan Opera Company was the leading opera company in the United States, and Anderson had dreamed of singing there since she was a young girl. At Hurok's invitation, Anderson and her husband attended the opera. Afterward, Anderson decided she would rather just skip the party and go home. But as they drove away, Anderson changed her mind. She told her husband, "I have a strange feeling that we should go to the party and say hello."[1] Fisher turned the car around and drove back to the party.

At the party, Rudolf Bing, general manager of the Metropolitan Opera Company, approached Anderson. He had a big question for her. Forgoing any small talk, he asked her point-blank if she would be interested in singing with the Metropolitan Opera Company. Anderson was stunned. No African American had ever performed in a major role with the Met in its seventy-year history. Anderson agreed to audition for a role in the opera *Un Ballo in Maschera* (The Masked Ball).

Anderson auditioned for the part with Dimitri Mitropoulos, the principal conductor of the Metropolitan Opera. The company wanted her to play the part of Ulrica, a fortune-teller in the opera. Anderson felt that the notes were too high for her. She sang the part and told Mitropoulos that she wanted to practice and return for another audition. But before she could reach home after the audition, Hurok had telephoned with congratulations. She got the part. At last, Anderson would make her opera debut.

Immediately, she called her husband and then her mother to share the good news. The Met's announcement that Anderson would perform in the opera, and thus break the color barrier, made national news. But as the excitement swirled around her, Anderson's professionalism took control and she got down to work. She had never performed in an operatic role before. Ulrica was a fortune-teller who made a short but dramatic appearance in the second scene of the first act. To master the role, Anderson spent hours in rehearsal with the conductor. She even rehearsed on Christmas Eve, New Year's Eve, and New Year's Day to prepare herself for the performance, which was scheduled for January 7, 1955.[2]

The day finally arrived for this momentous occasion. In the cold January air, at 5:30 A.M., people lined up for standing-room tickets for the sold-out performance.[3] Opera lovers flew in from all over the country, even from as far away as California. In the audience sat notable persons such as Ralph Bunche, the undersecretary of the United Nations; author Langston Hughes; English royalty the Duke and Duchess of Windsor; and Margaret Truman, the daughter of President Harry S. Truman. In the box seats sat Anderson's husband,

Orpheus "King" Fisher; her mother, Anna Anderson; her sisters, Alyce Anderson and Ethel Anderson DePreist; and her nephew, James Anderson DePreist.

Backstage, Anderson, in a long flowing costume and a long black wig, readied herself for the debut of her lifetime. Sol Hurok grasped her hand and said, "It won't be long now."[4]

Anderson replied, "Not as long as it has been."[5]

The first scene of the first act ended. Now the real drama was about to begin. The lights brightened, and the orchestra began to play. Just when the audience expected the gold-colored curtain to rise, the music stopped. Mistaken signals had caused the orchestra to begin too soon. The audience members, already on the edges of their seats, waited. The maestro, Dimitri Mitropoulous, signaled the orchestra to begin again. They played the introductory music to the end. Anticipation electrified the air. At last, the gold curtain rose like a golden sun rising on a new day. On the stage sat Anderson as Ulrica, the fortune-teller, stirring her brew in a witch's cauldron. The audience exploded with a standing ovation. This time the maestro stopped the music on purpose. Applause filled the hall. Then Anderson began to sing the aria.

Music reviewer Howard Taubman wrote, "Many in the audience knew that Miss Anderson—like Joshua but more quietly—had fought the battle of Jericho and at last the walls had come tumbling down."[6]

When the act ended, Anderson took her bows with the other performers. The audience applauded again and called her back for a number of bows. Although the policy at the Met forbade solo bows, an exception was made for this occasion, and Anderson took a solo bow amid cheers of "Bravo!"

Backstage, her dressing room overflowed with flowers and more than two thousand telegrams of congratulations. Anna Anderson told a reporter that she had hoped and dreamed for this day to come. She then kissed her daughter and said, "We thank the Lord."[7]

Many reviewers praised her performance. One critic wrote that she "had demonstrated the same musicianship and instinct for dramatic communication that she had long since demonstrated on the concert stage."[8]

Still, the reviewers also noted that Anderson, in her fifties, was past her prime for the part. One wrote, "There were those who wished this night had happened ten years earlier when the contralto was at her vocal peak. But this was not a performance to be judged as any other."[9]

A reporter asked Anderson about being the first African American to be featured with the Metropolitan Opera. Anderson responded, "I would say just this: I know that what happened tonight was not for me alone."[10]

A week following Anderson's debut, African-American singer Robert McFerrin, the father of singer/ musician Bobby McFerrin, joined the Metropolitan Opera Company. In time, other black singers joined the company as major performers.

Years later Anderson recalled:

I wanted to sing in opera. That was my dream. . . . If only I could give what I had to offer then. But they wouldn't accept it, or me. Other Negroes will have the career I dreamed of because this is one more barrier that's been let down.[11]

Over the next few years, she would open even more doors at home and abroad.

Chapter 9

AMBASSADOR AND DELEGATE

In 1955, while on a tour of North Africa, Anderson and her accompanist, Franz Rupp, visited the young nation of Israel. When Rupp's family had fled Adolf Hitler's Nazi Germany, they had moved to Israel. Anderson and Rupp visited them on a *kibbutz*, an Israeli communal farm. It was during the Passover holiday, and Anderson and Rupp attended a community seder. The seder is a traditional feast during which Jews recall the history of their people. Anderson had learned about Passover from her grandfather.

Anderson also visited the city of Jerusalem, the Jordan River, the walls of Jericho, and other biblical sites. Visiting places she had sung about in spirituals moved her deeply. Anderson knew that the slaves who created the spirituals had expressed their emotions and dreams in the terms that were closest to them—terms from the Bible. To create and sing those songs, she said, was an act of liberation, because they openly expressed the slaves' desire to escape their terrible conditions.[1]

Anderson had tea with the Israeli president, Itzhak Ben-Zvi, and performed with the Israel Philharmonic Orchestra. She was impressed with the role music played in the young nation. Recognizing musical talent in the Israeli youth, she responded in her usual generous manner and established a music scholarship fund there.

Back home at Marianna Farm, Anderson completed her autobiography, *My Lord, What a Morning*. She dedicated the book to her mother. It was published in 1956 to glowing reviews.

President Dwight D. Eisenhower was elected to a second term in 1956. Anderson sang the national anthem at his second inauguration in January 1957. The United States was then in what was called a "Cold War" with the Soviet Union. The two countries did not fight on the battlefields, but it was a time of great fear, distrust, and rivalry. The United States and the Soviet Union had different political and economic systems. The United States was a democracy, a capitalist country, and the Soviet Union was a communist country. Each country accused the other of trying to win over other nations and take over the world. One region of particular interest was Asia. The Soviet Union sent artists there to promote its cultural achievements. In response, the United States sent its artists. President Eisenhower asked Marian Anderson to become a "goodwill ambassador" for the United States, and she agreed.

In the fall of 1957, Anderson set out on a tour of twelve Asian countries that included South Korea, South Vietnam, Thailand, Burma, and India. Before she departed, the State Department instructed her just to be herself. Franz Rupp accompanied her.

Edward R. Murrow and a CBS television crew filmed the tour for his *See It Now* television series.

The journey of thirty-five thousand miles began with a visit to South Korea. Anderson flew in a helicopter to a hillside to sing for the five thousand American soldiers still stationed there after the Korean War. In 1950, North Korea had invaded South Korea in a surprise attack. Member nations of the United Nations, including the United States, sent troops to assist South Korea in the war. The war ended in 1953, but some of the U.S. troops remained. In the capital city of Seoul, Anderson was presented with an honorary degree from Ewha Women's University. The president of the university, Helen Kim, told her, "You are respected as a leader among women. Your success against great odds has encouraged others in their struggle for justice and human rights."[2] After receiving the degree, Anderson sang the spiritual "He's Got the Whole World in His Hands."

For the tour, Anderson chose the standard classics such as Schubert's "Ave Maria" and some of the spirituals she loved to sing. In Bangkok, Thailand, a grade-school child asked her to name her favorite song. Anderson replied that one of her favorite songs was the spiritual "Trampin'." She explained that the spirituals were born out of sadness and that the song "Trampin'" was about "walking along slowly and very hard because you have on your shoulders many unpleasant things."[3] She told the children about Abraham Lincoln and the Emancipation Proclamation.

In South Vietnam, which was in the midst of a civil war with North Vietnam, Anderson prayed and sang "Let My People Go." Although she was Christian, Anderson felt at home in other places of worship such as a Buddhist temple, a Jewish synagogue, or a

Muslim mosque. While in Rangoon, Burma, she told a Buddhist scholar, "Whether you call it one faith or another isn't too terribly important. What is important . . . [is] to do the very best it is in us to do."[4]

On the tour, Anderson sang and was sung to as well. In Saigon, South Vietnam, a group of schoolchildren greeted her with the song "Getting to Know You," from the musical *The King and I*. The children in the front row wore huge straw hats. The hats had music sheets attached them so that the children in the next row could read the lyrics.

Throughout the tour, her concerts drew thousands of people. Eight thousand people came to hear her sing in tiny Hong Kong.

Until Anderson's arrival in Delhi, India, no visiting foreign dignitary had ever been invited to speak at the Gandhi Memorial. Mahatma Gandhi was an Indian leader who led his people to freedom from British rule. Anderson was honored with an invitation to speak at the memorial. Before a gathering of several thousand Indians, she spoke about Gandhi: "Knowing some of the life and the inspiration of Mahatma Gandhi, as a Negro I was naturally very deeply moved and felt it absolutely imperative to come to this spot before returning to my own country."[5] She described his life as a shining beacon and asked the audience to bow their heads in his memory. She then led them in singing one of Gandhi's favorite hymns, "Lead, Kindly Light."

As she traveled, Anderson spread goodwill and the goodwill flowed back to her. Unfortunately, civil unrest was stirring in her own homeland, and it followed her like a shadow. In September 1957, the school board of Little Rock, Arkansas, agreed to admit a few black students into the all-white Central High School. In response, the governor, Orval Faubus, called out the National Guard to bar the students from entering the school. President Eisenhower sent in federal troops to force the students' entry. It was a tumultuous time.

Members of the press often tried to question Anderson about the racial unrest in her own country. Anderson responded by stating that she "felt grieved about it." Tactfully, she avoided making any statements that the press could turn into provocative headlines. She refused to engage in any long discussion because she felt it was neither the time nor the place to do so.[6]

The goodwill tour ended successfully. The documentary, entitled *The Lady from Philadelphia*, was broadcast on Murrow's *See It Now* series on December 30, 1957. It was one of the highest-rated shows of the year.

After the tour, the State Department presented Anderson with a citation that stated, "You have, in short, brought great credit to your country."[7]

Anderson's diplomatic skills did not go unnoticed by President Eisenhower. In 1958, he asked her to serve as a member of the United States delegation to the United Nations. The United Nations is an international organization established to ensure peace and cooperation among countries around the world. Each member nation sends delegates to the organization's General Assembly.

More comfortable as a musical performer, Marian Anderson accepted her new diplomatic role with some anxiety. But she also saw it as a way to build bridges of understanding among peoples around the world. The Asian tour had enlightened her about how little she knew of people in other lands and how ignorance led to misconceptions. Anderson stated, "Cities were dots on maps, far away. . . . Then one goes there and sees the buildings . . . and also talks to people as intelligent as one finds anywhere."[8]

On September 16, 1958, the thirteenth session of the United Nations General Assembly convened. Anderson, who had suspended her singing career during this time, entered her small office at 2 Park Avenue in New York City and simply said, "I like it here."[9] She was assigned to the Trusteeship Committee, which dealt with matters concerning territories that were under the supervision of the United Nations. These trust territories were home to more than 100 million people in Africa and the South Pacific. Anderson felt comfortable with her assignment. She said that she understood the hopes and demands of the small nations, particularly, those whose people were dark-skinned.[10] Anderson worked as hard at fulfilling her responsibilities as a delegate as she had as a performer.

Her commitment even led once to a disagreement with her own government. A proposal was presented to the Trusteeship Committee to hold a special General Assembly session to consider the future independence of two African trust territories, the British and the French Cameroons. The official United States position was that the subject did not warrant a special session. After Anderson presented the official United States position, she added a personal statement: "There is no one in this room who is more interested in the people whose fate we are trying to determine than I." She described herself as a member of "an instructed delegation."[11] In that way, Anderson made it clear that she disagreed with the official position of the United States. The consensus of the diplomats was that she had scored a personal triumph.

In the end, her diligent work and personal involvement helped to effect the independence of three African countries: the British and French Cameroons, and Togoland. In December, the session ended, and Anderson returned to her concert schedule. Henry Cabot Lodge, chief United States delegate to the United Nations, praised her work and called her a very effective member. In her usual dignified manner, Anderson had successfully influenced the organization.

In 1960, a new president was elected—John F. Kennedy. At his inauguration in January 1961, Anderson sang the "The Star Spangled Banner," as she had done for President Eisenhower. During Kennedy's presidency, Anderson helped to create the Freedom from Hunger Foundation. This organization, working with the United Nations, aimed to end world hunger. Anderson met with President Kennedy and West German Chancellor Konrad Adenauer at the White House to discuss the organization. She also performed at the White House in a concert.

In July 1963, Dr. Martin Luther King, Jr., led the national demonstration known as the March on Washington for Jobs and Freedom. Following the tradition begun by her 1939 concert, the march began at the Lincoln Memorial in Washington, D.C. Dr. King invited Marian Anderson to the march; she attended and sang a spiritual.

On November 22, 1963, President Kennedy was assassinated. Anderson had the sad duty to sing at a special memorial for him in New York City in December 1963. Standing before City Hall, she sang three spirituals in her soul-stirring way.

Before his death, President Kennedy had nominated Anderson for the Presidential Medal of Freedom, the nation's highest honor. A few weeks after the assassination, President Lyndon Johnson awarded Anderson the medal as members of Congress and the Supreme Court looked on.

Shortly after Marian Anderson received the award, Anna Anderson died at home in South Philadelphia in January 1964. Anderson accepted her mother's death in the strong, faithful way her mother had taught her. Anna Anderson's encouragement and guidance had enabled her daughter to have an outstanding career.

At last, though, the time had come for Anderson to say good-bye to the career that had brought her adoration all over the world.

Chapter 10

FAREWELL

"O ne more," said Sol Hurok, urging Anderson to take another bow after her final concert. "No," answered Anderson. "It's finished."[1]

On December 12, 1963, Marian Anderson had announced her farewell to the world. Her worldwide concert tours would come to an end after a farewell tour. It would begin in October 1964 in Washington, D.C., and end in April 1965 in New York City. Between those two concerts, she would perform in major cities on four continents. Emphasizing that her career was a "joyous, joyous time from the beginning to now," Anderson expressed a desire to pursue other interests. She explained that it was also important to "get into the field, and to be of service where there might be a need."[2] Some of the areas of deep concern to her involved children, particularly education and homelessness.

The farewell tour would end the yearly tours that placed her on a rigorous schedule of ten concerts a month. At age sixty-six,

Anderson knew that besides being unable to keep up such a strenuous schedule, her voice was no longer the powerful instrument it once was. Many people were reluctant to let her leave the stage. But Anderson knew it was time to go. She did not want people ever to say that they were sorry for her.

Ironically, the farewell tour began with a sold-out performance in Constitution Hall in Washington, D.C., the place where she had been barred from singing by the DAR in 1939. When asked if she had forgiven the organization, Anderson replied, "Ages and ages ago. You lose a lot of time hating people."[3]

At her farewell concert in her hometown of Philadelphia, the audience stood in tribute to her. A state representative called Anderson a great lady and a great credit to her native city. Family members and childhood friends watched her receive a floral tribute. A special event highlighted this concert. Anderson's nephew, James DePreist, had just won the 1964 Dimitri Mitropoulos International Conducting Competition. His Aunt Marian requested that he conduct the Philadelphia Orchestra at her Philadelphia farewell concert.

But it was at her final concert, in New York City on Easter Sunday, April 18, 1965, that the flowers and applause poured down on her. Dressed in a red satin gown with a wide mink collar, Marian Anderson stood on the Carnegie Hall stage. Her large brown eyes glistened as the audience, which had flowed onto the stage, clapped and cheered. During the intermission, she and her accompanist, Franz Rupp, were called back many times to take a bow. Bouquets of roses were thrust upon her. The program consisted of her favorites, including songs by Handel and Schubert and a group of spirituals. It ended with the all-time favorite, "He's Got the Whole

World in His Hands." After that, the audience did not want her to stop. She had to sing almost another concert of encores.

Finally, she left the stage with the roar of applause behind her. Laden with yellow roses and red chrysanthemums, she hurried to her dressing room. Telegrams of congratulations from all over the world covered her dressing table. Well-wishers crowded her room.

"They're still clapping, Miss Anderson," an usher called out.

"I had better go down again," Anderson said and went to take her final bow.[4]

The praise continued. The French government invited her to take part in the 1965 Festival of Negro Arts in Senegal, West Africa. In 1966, President Lyndon Johnson appointed her to the National Council on the Arts. In 1969, the National Association of Negro Musicians, Inc., honored her as the "singer of the century." And in 1973, she was elected to the National Women's Hall of Fame.

In America's bicentennial year, 1976, Anderson toured in composer Aaron Copland's *A Lincoln Portrait*. In her rich melodic voice, she read the words of Abraham Lincoln. On the Bicentennial Fourth of July, she also read the Declaration of Independence to President Gerald Ford.

In 1977, Anderson was one of the recipients of the *Ladies Home Journal*'s "Women of the Year" awards. Also, the year 1977 was celebrated as Anderson's seventy-fifth birthday year. (A birth certificate would be discovered after her death that established 1897 as her actual birth year.) A huge birthday celebration was held in her honor at Carnegie Hall in New York City. Dressed in a turquoise and orange African-inspired gown, a frail but elated Anderson rose from her box to acknowledge the standing ovation. Beside her, applauding, stood First Lady Rosalynn Carter. The songs on the program represented Anderson's distinguished career, including an aria from Giuseppe Verdi's *Un Ballo in Maschera* (The Masked Ball). African-American soprano Leontyne Price performed. Price had joined the Metropolitan Opera six years after Anderson's groundbreaking debut. She ended the program with "He's Got the Whole World in His Hands."

In the audience sat Rudolf Bing, who had brought Anderson to the Metropolitan Opera. Also present was Mayor Abraham Beame of New York City, who presented her with the city's Handel Medallion award. She also received the United Nations Peace Prize from the director of the United Nations Children's Fund. Mrs. Carter announced a congressional resolution, which authorized the Treasury Department to strike a gold medal in Anderson's honor. (The congressional gold medal was presented to Anderson by President Carter in October 1978.) Moved by the tribute, Anderson said, "Because there are so many friends here tonight, I feel compelled to tell you that I am profoundly happy."[5]

In keeping with her commitment to help children, the proceeds from the affair went to one of her favorite causes, Young Audiences, a nonprofit organization that sponsors programs in the arts for schoolchildren.

Anderson also worked with the Dance Theater of Harlem, an African-American ballet company that draws its young dancers from New York's inner city. A long time had passed since Anderson had tried to stand on her toes. For a benefit performance, Anderson, accompanied by a nurse, read a specially prepared text about the roots of spiritual music.

In April 1977, Anderson donated her personal papers and other memorabilia, such as photographs and awards, to the University of

Pennsylvania. On that occasion marked by music and tributes, Anderson told the audience, "To all of you here, to the mothers and grandmothers of some of you who gave me a nudge during my career. . . . I thank you for all of the things that have happened."[6] Her nephew, James DePreist, an alumnus of the University of Pennsylvania, escorted her to the celebration.

In December 1978, the John F. Kennedy Center for the Performing Arts in Washington, D.C., presented its first annual awards for "lifetime achievements in the arts." Marian Anderson was an honoree at this grand occasion along with dancer Fred Astaire, choreographer George Balanchine, composer Richard Rodgers, and pianist Arthur Rubinstein. Anderson's trademark spiritual, "He's Got the Whole World in His Hands," was sung by Aretha Franklin and the Howard University Choir.

By the 1980s, the elderly singer remained mostly at home on her farm in Connecticut, tending to her ailing husband. Orpheus Fisher had suffered a stroke and was unable to speak.

Still, the public would not let her be. On January 31, 1982, a celebration honoring Anderson's eightieth birthday was held at Carnegie Hall. Two African-American sopranos, Shirley Verrett and Grace Bumbry, acknowledged their indebtedness to Anderson with a joyous tribute. Both singers had entered opera after Anderson broke the color line, and both had been recipients of the Marian Anderson Scholarship Award. After a birthday message from President Ronald Reagan, the packed crowd broke into "Happy Birthday, Dear Marian."

In 1984, the mayor of New York presented Anderson with the first Eleanor Roosevelt Human Rights Award of the City of New York. A tearful Anderson, by then confined to a wheelchair, stated,

"I have thanked my good Lord for her [Eleanor Roosevelt] many times. I am only sorry the youngsters of today shall not have seen her in the flesh."[7]

In March 1986, Anderson's husband, Orpheus "King" Fisher, died.

In 1987, the University of Connecticut awarded her an honorary doctor of letters degree. Even as a woman in her nineties, Anderson remained involved in helping young people. She helped establish the Marian Anderson Award in Danbury, Connecticut, to help promising singers. (The Marian Anderson Scholarship Award established in 1941 had ceased functioning in 1970.) In August 1989, a concert was held at the Charles Ives Center for the Arts in Danbury to raise funds for the award. Soprano Jessye Norman, violinist Isaac Stern, and the Ives Symphony Orchestra performed. Anderson was presented with bouquets of flowers and a message of praise from President George Bush.

Anderson also worked with the Girl Scouts of America and other charitable organizations such as the American Red Cross and the Spence-Chapin Adoption Service. Her contributions were made privately because she did not believe in making a public show of her generosity.

In interviews, Anderson often referred to herself as "we." Once she was asked why she said *we* instead of *I*. Anderson replied:

> Possibly because the longer one lives, one realizes that there is no particular thing that you can do alone. . . . there are many people—those who wrote the music, those who made the pianos on which the accompanist is playing, the accompanist who actually lends support to the performance. . . . So the "I" in it is very small after all.[8]

In 1992, an ailing Anderson left Marianna Farm to live with her nephew, James DePreist, in Portland, Oregon.

On April, 8, 1993, at age ninety-six, Marian Anderson died of congestive heart failure. She was buried in Eden Cemetery in Collingdale, Pennsylvania. Her obituary appeared in newspapers nationwide. On her passing, one writer wrote: "Not until 1955 . . . was she given the opportunity to make her Metropolitan Opera debut. What she might have achieved if that chance had come earlier remains a question. In its answer lies one reason that America remembers her with such a hopeless tangle of pride and shame."[9]

On June 7, 1993, a memorial service was held at Carnegie Hall in New York. When Anderson had discussed with her nephew a memorial service for her, she told him, "Jim, don't let them make a big fuss. And no speeches."[10] At the memorial, four portraits of Anderson were suspended over the stage. A piano stood center stage with a display of large floral pieces. There were no speeches. Fourteen of her recordings were played, including her favorites, "Ave Maria" and "He's Got the Whole World in His Hands." At the end of the last recording, the audience responded with a standing ovation.

The standing ovation has continued in tributes of words and deeds in the years that followed.

Chapter 11

REMEMBERING THE LADY FROM PHILADELPHIA

Tributes in various ways were made to Anderson after her death. On February 3, 1994, an event honoring Anderson was held on the City College campus of the City University of New York. On that occasion, the main auditorium of Aaron Davis Hall was renamed the Marian Anderson Theater. The building, erected in 1979, occupies the site of the former Lewisohn Stadium, where Anderson had sung with the New York Philharmonic Orchestra.

At the affair, for which First Lady Hillary Rodham Clinton was the honorary chairperson, the performers included jazz drummer Max Roach, author Maya Angelou, and the Dance Theater of Harlem. Showcased were eleven of Anderson's gowns, which were later displayed at the Museum of the City of New York. The gowns were donated by singer Bette Midler, who had acquired them at an auction.[1]

On February 27, 1997, Carnegie Hall staged a hundredth-anniversary tribute to Marian Anderson. The Morgan State

University Choir performed, along with mezzo-soprano Denyce Graves of the Metropolitan Opera. Some of the speakers included poet laureate Rita Dove and Anderson's nephew, James DePreist. Accompanying the tribute was a three-month exhibition of Anderson memorabilia at the Rose Museum at the hall.[2]

Monetary awards were established to honor Anderson as well. In 1998, Mayor Edward G. Rendell announced the city of Philadelphia's Marian Anderson Award, named in honor of its native daughter. The award was established to celebrate artists who used their talents for the betterment of society. The first recipient of the award was Harry Belafonte, the world-renowned entertainer and social activist. The award, with its cash prize of $100,000, was presented to Belafonte in June 1998.

The Marian Anderson Award Foundation located in Danbury, Connecticut, grants an annual award to a mid-career American singer. Anderson wanted the award bestowed on an accomplished singer whose career might be in need of a boost. The winner is selected from singers who have been nominated by music professionals such as conductors or artistic directors. A panel of retired singers, conductors, and accompanists reviews the tapes submitted by the nominees and then selects the winner.

The Van Pelt-Dietrich Library at the University of Pennsylvania received a grant from the National Endowment for the Humanities to organize the Anderson collection, which include letters, taped interviews, news clippings, diaries, and photographs. During the process of organizing the collection, the library discovered a handwritten manuscript by the Finnish composer Jean Sibelius, who had told Anderson that his roof was too low for her voice. Also discovered was a 1936 recording of "War det en drom" ("Was It a Dream") that had never been commercially released.

The library also has established a Marian Anderson Music Study Center as a living memorial to her. The center, which opened in October 1998, is a large facility designed to meet the needs of the students and faculty in their music research. The center has changing exhibits on Anderson's career and provides access to her recordings.

In addition, the library has online a multimedia exhibition of Anderson's life, "Marian Anderson: A Life in Song." The exhibition can be accessed on the Internet.

Anderson chose not to have children because of the extensive traveling her career required. But she was beloved by her nephew and godson, James Anderson DePreist. As a young man, DePreist enrolled at the University of Pennsylvania with an interest in studying law. In his senior year, he led a hundred-piece student band. His aunt often gave him classical records to listen to, and apparently they had an effect on him. He enrolled in the Philadelphia Conservatory of Music. After DePreist won the Mitropoulos International Conducting Competition, conductor Leonard Bernstein appointed him assistant conductor of the New York Philharmonic Orchestra. DePreist went on to conduct abroad in numerous places, among them Italy, France, Australia, and the Far East. Later, he became the music director and conductor of the Oregon Symphony in Portland.

Reflecting on his famous aunt, Maestro DePreist stated that, unfortunately, social issues such as the DAR incident overshadowed his aunt's tremendous talent and artistry. As an example, he noted that her Metropolitan Opera debut actually occurred when she was five years older than everyone thought, because she was born in 1897 and not in 1902, as was believed at the time. Therefore, her opera debut took place one month before her fifty-eighth birthday, which is an extraordinary achievement for an opera singer.[3]

DePreist also stated that despite her worldwide fame, his aunt never forgot her roots. Anderson loved children a great deal, he said. He recalled one Christmas in the 1940s when Anderson threw a party for the children in her South Philadelphia neighborhood. For the occasion, she purchased hundreds of dolls—tall black dolls with moving eyes—for the girls and footballs for the boys. DePreist remembered the event because the leftover toys were stored in his basement, and as a result of the Christmas party, he always had an extra supply of footballs.[4]

DePreist acknowledged his aunt's legacy in his own career and how the barriers she broke are now taken for granted. He recalled an experience conducting at Constitution Hall in Washington, D.C., the same hall that had barred his aunt from performing. DePreist said, "It was so simple for me. I just parked the car, went in the stage door, came onstage, rehearsed, and then returned to the hotel. None of those things was my aunt able to do in 1939. I called her as soon as I got back to the hotel. I told her what I had just done, and I said, 'It's incredible to me that there was a time when you were not able to do those things.'"[5] Marian Anderson simply replied that she was "just grateful that things had changed."[6]

This great lady, who entertained kings and queens with the same grace she entertained neighborhood children, broke down barriers and endured indignities during a career that spanned four decades. She may have received the keys to Atlantic City, New Jersey, but she found no hotel there that would accept her for the night. She may have stayed in other hotels on her tours, but she had to use the freight elevators to get to her room. Some people wanted her to be more vocal and more visible in the civil rights movement. But she stayed true to her course.

Anderson perfected her art, quietly raised funds at home for civil rights organizations, and demanded that her audiences be integrated even if the nation was not. Her legacy was aptly described by singer Leontyne Price: "Marian Anderson's superb professional triumphs were only a small part of what this great diva contributed to human understanding. As a nation, we owe her gratitude for showing that talent and dignity can prevail and wrongs can be corrected."[7]

CHRONOLOGY

1897—Marian Anderson is born in Philadelphia, Pennsylvania, on February 27.

1903—Begins singing with the Union Baptist Church.

1910—Her father, John Anderson, dies.

1915—Begins voice lessons under Mary Patterson.

1920—Begins voice lessons with Giuseppe Boghetti.

1923—Wins first prize in Philadelphia Philharmonic Society vocal contest.

1924—Gives Town Hall recital in New York City.

1925—Wins National Music League contest; sings with New York Philharmonic Orchestra.

1928—Makes first trip to Europe.

1931—Returns to Europe on an award from the Julius Rosenwald Fund; meets accompanist Kosti Vehanen.

1932—Performs in Norway, Sweden, and Finland.

1933—Returns to Europe for a two-year concert tour.

1935—Signs with impresario Sol Hurok; meets celebrated conductor Arturo Toscanini; gives successful Town Hall concert on return to the United States.

1936—Performs in the Soviet Union; performs at the White House.

1938—Performs in South America.

1939—Gives Lincoln Memorial Concert on April 9 after being barred from Constitutional Hall by the Daughters of the American Revolution; is invited to the White House to sing for King George VI and Queen Elizabeth; receives the Spingarn Medal from the NAACP.

1941—Wins Philadelphia's Bok Award; establishes scholarship fund for young singers.

1943—Marries Orpheus "King" Fisher; awarded the Liberian Order of African Redemption from Liberia.

1946—Receives the Order of the White Rose from Finland.

1952—Receives the Litteris et Artibus medal from Sweden.

1955—Becomes the first African American to sing in New York City's Metropolitan Opera Company in a featured role.

1956—Publishes autobiography, *My Lord, What a Morning.*

1957—Sings the national anthem at second inauguration of President Dwight D. Eisenhower; tours the Far East as a "goodwill" ambassador.

1958—Serves as United States delegate to the United Nations.

1961—Sings the national anthem at inauguration of President John F. Kennedy.

1963—Receives the Presidential Medal of Freedom.

1964—Her mother, Anna Anderson, dies.

1965—Retires from concert singing after a worldwide farewell tour.

1976—Tours in Aaron Copeland's *A Lincoln Portrait.*

1977—Celebrates seventy-fifth birthday at Carnegie Hall; receives United Nations Peace Prize.

1978—Receives Lifetime Achievement in the Arts award at Kennedy Center; receives congressional gold medal from President Jimmy Carter.

1982—Celebrates eightieth birthday at Carnegie Hall.

1986—Husband Orpheus "King" Fisher dies.

1993—Marian Anderson dies on April 8.

MUSIC BY MARIAN ANDERSON

A Selected Discography

Brahms; Alto Rhapsody/ Anderson, Ormandy, Philadelphia Orchestra (Pearl, 1992)

Marian Anderson Vol. 1—Bach, Handel, Schubert, Brahm (Pearl, 1992)

Jascha Horenstein—The Complete Paris Concert of 11/22/56 (Music & Arts, 1993)

The Lady from Philadelphia—Marian Anderson (Pearl, 1993)

Tribute to Marian Anderson (Pro Arte, 1993)

Marian Anderson—Bach, Brahms, Schubert (BMG/RCA Victor, 1994)

Spirituals (Pearl Flapper, 1995)

Prima Voce—Marian Anderson—Spirituals, Oratorio Excerpts (Nimbus, 1997)

Favorite Christmas Hymns (BMG/RCA Special Products, 1998)

Marian Anderson: Rare and Unpublished Recordings, 1936–1952 (VAI Audio, 1998)

Recordings from 1936–1947, Vol. 2 (Nimbus, 1998)

Spirituals (BMG/RCA Victor, 1999)

CHAPTER NOTES

Chapter 1. Town Hall—A Leap Forward

1. Sol Hurok, with Ruth Goode, *Impresario, A Memoir* (New York: Random House, 1946), p. 242.

2. Marian Anderson, *My Lord, What a Morning* (New York: Viking Press, 1956), p. 165.

3. Ibid., p. 76.

4. Hurok, p. 242.

5. Rosalyn M. Story, *And So I Sing: African-American Divas of Opera and Concert* (New York: Warner Books, 1990), p. 47.

6. Ibid.

7. "Marian Anderson in Concert Here," *The New York Times*, December 31, 1935.

8. Anderson, p. 169.

Chapter 2. Baby Contralto

1. Marian Anderson, "Grace Before Greatness," *Guideposts*, March 1954, p. 2.

2. "Marian Anderson, 96, Dies; Singer Who Broke Barriers," *The New York Times*, April 9, 1993, p. 20. [*Author's note*: Marian Anderson gave her birth date as February 17, 1902. After her death, a birth certificate was discovered stating that she was born on February 27, 1897.]

3. Barbara Klaw, "Interview with Marian Anderson," *American Heritage*, February 1977.

4. Ibid.

5. Felicia Warburg Roosevelt, *Doers & Dowagers* (New York: Doubleday & Company, Inc., 1975), p. 141.

6. Darlene Clark Hine, *Facts on File Encyclopedia of Black Women in America* (New York: Facts on File, Inc., 1997), p. 45.

7. Anderson, "Grace Before Greatness," p. 3.

8. Emily Kimbrough, "My Life in a White World," *Ladies Home Journal*, September 1960, p. 54.

9. Ibid.

10. Roosevelt, p. 144.

11. James Weldon Johnson, *The Book of American Negro Spirituals* (New York: Viking Press, 1925), p. 20.

12. Klaw.

13. Marian Anderson, *My Lord, What a Morning* (New York: Viking Press, 1956), p. 29.

14. Ibid. p. 46.

Chapter 3. Singing Lessons

1. Marian Anderson, *My Lord, What a Morning* (New York: Viking Press, 1956), p. 47.

2. Ibid., p. 62.

3. Barbara Klaw, "Interview with Marian Anderson," *American Heritage*, February 1977.

4. Anderson, p. 41.

5. Edwin R. Embree, *Thirteen Against the Odds* (New York: Viking Press, 1944), p. 145.

6. Anderson, p. 53.

7. Ibid., pp. 77–78.

8. Sol Hurok, with Ruth Goode, *Impresario, A Memoir* (New York: Random House, 1946), pp. 246–247.

9. "Review," cited in Kosti Vehanen, *Marian Anderson, A Portrait* (Westport, Conn.: Greenwood Press, 1970), p. 259.

10. Anderson, p. 109.

11. "Marian Anderson," in Maxine Black, ed., *Current Biography Who's News and Why 1940* (New York: The H. W. Wilson Company, 1940), p. 18.

12. Anderson, p. 112.

13. Ibid., p. 114.

Chapter 4. "Marian Fever" Abroad

1. Marian Anderson, *My Lord, What a Morning* (New York: Viking Press, 1956), p. 119.

2. Ibid., pp. 121–124.

3. Ibid., p. 125.

4. Jesse Carney Smith, ed., *Notable Black American Women* (Detroit: Gale Research Inc., 1992), p. 15.

5. Kosti Vehanen, *Marian Anderson, A Portrait* (Westport, Conn.: Greenwood Press, 1970), p. 20.

6. Roy De Coverly, "Marian Anderson in Denmark," *Opportunity*, September 1934, pp. 270–271.

7. Anderson, p. 145.

8. Ibid., p. 148.

9. Edwin R. Embree, *13 Against the Odds* (New York: Viking Press, 1944), pp. 146–147.

10. Sol Hurok, with Ruth Goode, *Impresario, A Memoir* (New York: Random House, 1946), p. 238.

Chapter 5. Once in a Hundred Years

1. Marian Anderson, *My Lord, What a Morning* (New York: Viking Press, 1956), p. 156.

2. Lindsay Patterson, ed., *International Library of Afro-American Life and History* (Cornwells Heights, Penn.: The Publishers Agency, Inc., 1976), p. 158.

3. Jessie Carney Smith, ed., *Notable Black American Women* (Detroit: Gale Research, Inc., 1992), p. 16.

4. Pitts Sanborn, "Ovation Won by Contralto at Carnegie," *New York World-Telegram*, March 10, 1936.

5. Kosti Vehanen, *Marian Anderson, A Portrait* (Westport, Conn.: Greenwood Press, 1970), pp. 71–72.

6. Anderson, p. 178.

7. Frank Merkling, "Marian Anderson: Another Milestone," *The News-Times* (Danbury, Conn.), February 21, 1982, p. E-5.

8. Vehanen, pp. 185–186.

9. Ibid., p. 201.

Chapter 6. An Easter Sunday Concert

1. Sol Hurok with Ruth Goode, *Impresario, A Memoir* (New York: Random House, 1946), p. 255.

2. Ibid., p. 257.

3. "Artists Assail D.A.R.'s Ban on Miss Anderson," *New York Herald Tribune*, February 23, 1939.

4. "Mrs. Roosevelt Hints She Quits D.A.R. Over Anderson Ban," *New York World-Telegram*, February 27, 1939.

5. "D.A.R. Tells Why It Barred Miss Anderson," *New York Herald Tribune*, April, 19, 1939.

6. Hurok, p. 255.

7. Kosti Vehanen, *Marian Anderson, A Portrait* (Westport, Conn.: Greenwood Press, 1970), p. 238.

8. Rosalyn M. Story, *And So I Sing* (New York: Warner Books, Inc., 1990), p. 51.

9. Marian Anderson, *My Lord, What a Morning* (New York: Viking Press, 1956), p. 189.

10. "75,000 Acclaim Miss Anderson; Easter Visitors Throng Capital," *The Washington Post*, April 10, 1939, p. 12.

11. "Throng Honors Marian Anderson in Concert at Lincoln Memorial," *The New York Times*, April 11, 1939.

12. Keith D. Miller and Emily M. Lewis, "Touchstones, Authorities, and Marian Anderson: The Making of 'I Have a Dream,'" in Brian Ward and Tony Badger, ed., *The Making of Martin Luther King and the Civil Rights Movement* (London: Macmillan Press Ltd., 1996), pp. 147, 150.

13. Ibid., p. 154.

14. Vehanen, pp. 233–234.

15. "First Lady Honors Marian Anderson," *The New York Times*, July 3, 1939.

Chapter 7. Married Life

1. William G. Nunn, "Marian Anderson Married," *The Pittsburgh Courier*, November 20, 1943, p. 1.

2. Ibid., p. 4.

3. Richard C. Wald, "To Him, Marian Anderson Is 'Angel,'" *New York Herald Tribune*, March 18, 1958, p. 3.

4. Ibid.

5. Emily Kimbrough, "My Life in a White World," *Ladies Home Journal*, September 1960, p. 174.

6. Ibid., p. 176.

7. Bill Ryan, "Serene Marian Anderson Lives on Danbury Farm," *The Hartford Times*, May 5, 1964.

8. Wald, p. 3.

9. Edwin R. Embree, *Thirteen Against the Odds* (New York: Viking Press, 1944), p. 151.

10. Kimbrough, p. 174.

11. Ibid.

12. Ibid.

13. Ibid.

14. "Mixed Miami Throng Hears Miss Anderson," *The New York Times*, January 26, 1953.

Chapter 8. A Dream Comes True

1. Marian Anderson, *My Lord, What a Morning* (New York: Viking Press, 1956), p. 295.

2. "Stranger at 'The Met,'" *Newsweek*, January 17, 1955.

3. Howard Taubman, "Marian Anderson Wins Ovation in First Opera Role at the 'Met,'" *The New York Times*, January 8, 1955, p. 11.

4. Louis Biancolli, "Miss Anderson's Debut at Met a Joy to Mother," *New York World-Telegram*, January 8, 1955, p. 1.

5. Ibid.

6. Taubman, p. 11.

7. Biancolli, p. 1.

8. Olin Downes, "Opera: 'Masked Ball' Given at Met," *The New York Times*, January 9, 1955.

9. "Stranger at 'The Met.'"

10. Biancolli, p. 2.

11. Kimbrough, p. 174.

Chapter 9. Ambassador and Delegate

1. Marian Anderson, *My Lord, What a Morning* (New York: Viking Press, 1956), pp. 261–262.

2. Edward R. Murrow, *The Lady From Philadelphia*, CBS-TV, December 30, 1957.

3. Ibid.

4. Ibid.

5. Ibid.

6. J. P. Shanley, "Singing Diplomat," *The New York Times*, December 29, 1957.

7. "Marian Anderson Receives Citation From State Dept.," *The New York Herald Tribune*, April 1, 1958, p. 17.

8. Harold Schonberg, "The Other Voice of Marian Anderson," *The New York Times*, August 10, 1958, p. 17.

9. "New Voice at the U.N.," *The New York Times*, September 18, 1958.

10. Emily Kimbrough, "My Life in a White World," *Ladies Home Journal*, September 1960, p. 176.

11. "Marian Anderson Acts Loyal Dissenter Role," *The New York Herald Tribune*, November 26, 1958.

Chapter 10. Farewell

1. Jimmy Breslin, "They're Still Clapping, Miss Anderson," *The New York Herald Tribune*, April 19, 1965, p. 1.

2. John Molleson, "Marian Anderson's Last Tour," *The New York Herald Tribune*, December 13, 1963.

3. Ibid.

4. Breslin, p. 25.

5. Anna Quindlen, "Marian Anderson Honored at 75 by Carnegie Hall Concert," *The New York Times*, February 28, 1977, p. 24.

6. Steve Stecklow, "Marian Anderson Returns with Memories, Thanks," *The Evening Bulletin* (Philadelphia), April 14, 1977, p. 40.

7. "Sentimental Ceremony for Marian Anderson," *The New York Times*, July 26, 1984.

8. Edwin R. Murrow, *The Lady From Philadelphia*, CBS-TV, December 30, 1957.

9. Anthony Heilbut, "Marian Anderson," *The New Yorker*, April 21, 1993.

10. Allan Kozinn, "A Tribute to Marian Anderson, For the Most Part in Her Voice," *The New York Times*, June 8, 1993.

Chapter 11. Remembering the Lady from Philadelphia

1. James R. Oestreich, "A Chorus of Strong Voices Recalls The Pure Force of Marian Anderson," *The New York Times*, February 5, 1994.

2. Peter G. Davis, "American Classics," *New York Magazine*, March 17, 1997, p. 84.

3. Personal interview with James DePreist, February 17, 1999.

4. Ibid.

5. David Lander, "Aunt Marian," *American Legacy*, Fall 1996, p. 34.

6. Ibid.

7. G. S. Bourdain, ed., "Professionally, Anderson Was 'the Mother of Us All,'" *The New York Times*, April 18, 1993, p. 23.

FURTHER READING

Books

Anderson, Marian. *My Lord, What a Morning.* New York: Viking Press, 1956. Reissue edition: University of Wisconsin Press, 1993.

Ferris, Jeri. *What I Had Was Singing.* Minneapolis: Carolrhoda Books, Inc., 1994.

Freedman, Russell. *The Voice That Challenged a Nation: Marian Anderson and the Struggle for Equal Rights.* New York: Clarion Books, 2004.

Jones, Victoria Garrett. *Marian Anderson: A Voice Uplifted.* New York: Sterling, 2008.

Osborne, Linda Barrett. *Miles to Go for Freedom: Segregation and Civil Rights in the Jim Crow Years.* New York: Harry N. Abrams, 2012.

INDEX